MW01233960

William the Conqueror

The last Viking

OREP Éditions, Zone tertiaire de Nonant, 14400 BAYEUX
Tel.: 02 31 51 81 31 – Fax: 02 31 51 81 32
E-mail: info@orepeditions.com – **Web:** www.orepeditions.com

Editor: Grégory Pique – **Design:** Éditions OREP
Editorial coordination: Corine Desprez
English translation: Heather Inglis

Graphics, layout: Noir O Blanc
Front cover Illustration: Paul Gastine
Back cover illustration: Photographs: Yohann Deslandes © Musée-Métropole-Rouen-Normandie

Vincent Carpentier

William the Conqueror

The last Viking

OREP
EDITIONS

This book has been actively supported by the members and friends of the association "Un fleuve pour la Liberté, la Dives".

I thank them most sincerely, as I do all the subscribers who have accompanied and trusted in me over this new adventure.

CONTENTS

Dives 1066

In 1064, the English King Edward the Confessor sent Harold Godwinson, the highest-ranking Anglo-Saxon lord, to Normandy, very probably to officially inform William the Bastard that he had chosen him as his successor. The event marks the opening scene of the Bayeux "tapestry", an extraordinary medieval masterpiece believed to have been produced in England around 1070-1080, upon orders by Odo of Bayeux, the Conqueror's half-brother. The ship transporting Harold and his court left Sussex and was most probably set off course by bad weather, to finally land on the Ponthieu coast in the Boulonnais region rather than in Normandy. Harold and his court were captured by the local count Guy's men, later to be released to William in exchange for a ransom. Following this unfortunate episode, the English court stayed for a while in Rouen, relishing in William's hospitality before accompanying the ducal army on a military expedition in Brittany. After the campaign, William symbolically embraced Harold, which may have been a form of dubbing, since knighthood did not yet exist at the time in England. Then the two noblemen returned to

Harold's oath. Scene 23 from the Bayeux Tapestry.

Normandy, side by side. Hence began the key event depicted on the tapestry: William had Harold solemnly swear on holy relics that, when the time came, he would respect his right to Edward's throne. Godwin's son then returned to England, accompanied by his young nephew Hakon who had, since his childhood, resided with the Norman court.

We all know what followed. When, on the 6th of January 1066, the pious King of England passed away, Harold, who was Godwin's eldest son, immediately had himself proclaimed king by the *Witan,* an assembly of English noblemen, then crowned in Westminster Abbey by Stigand, the Archbishop of Canterbury. Could he have forced a belated appointment from the dying king? Whatever... he was guilty of perjury and was now to face his fate.

It is unlikely that William was truly surprised to learn the news that was brought to him by a crew of sailors – spies shall we say – posted in England. He immediately set to organising his military campaign which appeared to augur well. Indeed, the tapestry depicts the amazement of the English people as they watch an unknown star sparkling in the sky; it was in fact Halley's comet, during its very first appearance recorded in history. Yet, William and Harold were not the only ones to play a role in the story. The English throne was also coveted by another far from insignificant peer: the King of Norway himself, Harald Hardraada (the "hard ruler"), also nicknamed the "Lightning of the North" and considered by many historians as the very last king of the Viking era. Harald, who had occupied the throne of Norway for twenty years, was a distinguished warrior. He had served in the East during the famous Byzantine Varangian Guard and had married a descendant of Rurik, the founding prince of Kievan Rus' – of which we will speak in more detail later. As such, his reputation stretched from the British Isles to Constantinople! It was most likely Harold's younger brother Tostig, consumed with ambition, who convinced Harald to claim the throne of England. He based his claim on a pact, said to have been sealed in 1038 or 1039, between the Danish King Canute the Great - at the time in control of England - and the Norwegian King Magnus, who was also Harald's nephew. In accordance with this pact, it was understood that if one were to die, the other would succeed him. Yet, Canute the Great passed away before Magnus and with no heir. As such, Harald, as Magnus's uncle, was in a position to claim his due.

William ordering the construction of the fleet and carpenters felling trees and building boats in Dives. Scene 35 from the Bayeux Tapestry.

As early as January 1066, William the Bastard ordered for his carpenters to build a fleet. The tapestry illustrates one of these men - most likely the ducal fleet's admiral - standing on William's right with a doloire in his hand: a long and narrow iron hatchet used to shape the planking. The duke's pointed finger on the same scene, signifies his order to take action. Without delay, his men gathered in a forest near the waterside, very probably located in Dives-sur-Mer, on the hillside that over-looks either side of the estuary which, at the time, was populated with oak and elm trees. These vast wooded areas belonged to the duke and his most faithful barons. The naval carpenters chopped down the high trees, then cut the pieces of wood to build boats directly on site, using green timber, which was common Scandinavian practice. This supple wood was rapidly assembled and the boats launched in the nearby estuary. The naval construction site is described in detail on the tapestry. Carpenters are seen using different tools: their doloires, hatchets, augers and hammers are all identical to those found by archaeologists on Scandinavian sites dating from the Viking Age. This similarity, along with many other details, proves that the tapestry is an exceptionally accurate source.

So it was the availability of a sufficient stock of wood and the proximity with a vast dry harbour that motivated the choice of the small Dives estuary to gather the ducal fleet. In addition, the area offered further logistic facilities in terms of shelters, warehouses, fodder supply for horses and foodstuffs for men, thanks to the nearby abbeys in Troarn and Caen, both founded by the duke or his closest barons during the 1050s and 1060s. At the time, the Dives estuary was subjected to greater tidal changes than it is today. The Cabourg headland did not yet exist and, at high tide, the river's waters were mixed with the sea to form a vast natural harbour, sheltered from the wind and surrounded by the villages of Dives-sur-Mer, Périers-en-Auge, Varaville and Cabourg. At the mouth of the river, there was a small harbour town dating, at least, back to the Roman period: Dives-sur-Mer, at the time referred to as Pont-Dives. For there is indeed mention of a bridge in 9th century documents, along with mills, salt mines, fisheries, cultivated fields and or-chards... William the Bastard was at home here. In 1057, he had won the Battle of Varaville thanks to the tidal effect on the Dives and its bridge. His castles in Caen and Bonneville-sur-Touques were close at hand and the boats could travel from Pont-Dives to the port of Caen. Finally, he had many faithful and powerful followers in the area, including

Dives church.

the Viscount of Hiémois, Roger the Great de Montgomery. The River Dives was, indeed, an essential navigable link between the estuary port and the inland area of Hiémois, William's family cradle. Falaise, the capital of this area, was his childhood home.

Without delay, the ships that had been built on the hillside were taken to the shore and launched, ready to sail. From the square spire of the Church of Notre-Dame in Dives, William contemplated his army... In the summer of 1066, the estuary welcomed a highly diverse fleet comprised of many ships of all sizes, requisitioned from ports throughout the duchy or specially built for the occasion. A total of around a thousand boats waited for their loads, their sails and their sculpted figureheads in true Viking tradition! The new ships William needed were most likely those that would be used to transport horses, a purpose for which local fleets were not suited. The "Ship List" is an extraordinary document, apparently drafted in Fécamp, detailing the fleet provided by the leading Norman barons and by the duke himself.

The Ship List mentions a total of 677 ships, including the *Mora*, equipped by Matilda. The fleet comprised many other vessels, which were requisitioned or provided by vassals of lesser rank. Let's not forget how costly it was in the 11th century to arm a horseman. It is because of this cost, and that of the boats themselves, that the list was compiled, along with its contribution scale. It was very probably used later to calculate the reward to be attributed to each participant during

Aerial view of the Dives estuary.

the distribution of acquired English territories. Whatever its many uses, the document offers unique proof of the probable existence of military and naval conscription in ducal Normandy, as attested by a few rare documents found in England and dating from the same period. Whatever, the exact number of ships that comprised William's fleet has been a great subject of debate. The Ship List mentions a total of 677 boats; yet, later in the same text, a thousand are mentioned. 12th century historians offer varying estimations. For example, Wace, in his *Roman de Rou*, writes that, according to his father's memories, a total of 696 ships entered Saint-Valery, 4 having been wrecked between Dives and the Pays de Caux, i.e. an original total of 700. In sharp contrast, William of Jumièges talks of a fleet of 3,000 boats! It appears that, finally, the figures on the List, which were more or less repeated by Wace, are the most convincing. The difference in the number of ships provided by noblemen (677) and the total of one thousand mentioned later may simply refer to the remainder provided by the duke himself from his own estates, including the lower Dives and nearby forests, i.e. some 300 ships.

The Ship List

"William, duke of the Normans, coming to England to take power, received, as was his right, from the Seneschal William FitzOsbern, 60 ships. As many from Hugh of Avranches, who later became the Earl of Chester. From Hugh of Montfort, 50 ships and 50 horsemen. From Rémi of Fécamp, chaplain, who later became Bishop of Lincoln, 1 ship with 20 horsemen. From Nicolas, Abbot of Saint-Ouen, 15 ships with 100 horsemen. From Robert, Count of Eu, 60 ships. From Fulk d'Aunou, 40 ships. As many from Gerold the Seneschal. From William, Count of Évreux, 80 ships. From Roger the Great de Montgomery, 60 ships. From Roger of Beaumont, 60 ships. From Odo, Bishop of Bayeux, 100 ships. From Robert of Mortain, 120. From Gautier Giffard, 30 ships with 100 horsemen. Over and above the aforementioned, which totalled around a thousand vessels, the duke received other ships from his men, each contributing within his means. The duke's wife Matilda, who later became queen, had a ship named *Mora* built in his honour and upon which the duke personally sailed. The same Matilda had a gilded statue of a small child placed at the prow of this ship; with his right hand, the child pointed towards England whilst his left hand held an ivory horn to his mouth. For this, the duke offered Matilda the County of Kent."

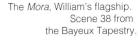

The *Mora*, William's flagship.
Scene 38 from
the Bayeux Tapestry.

As for the type of ship provided, they were, in all evidence, very similar to the large Scandinavian ships common to the Viking Age. Although archaeological wrecks dating from the period are extremely rare, several ship elements have been found in the port of London, offering evidence of the existence of Scandinavian ships in England in the 11th century. So, it would appear that those used in the English Channel at the time were very much inspired by Scandinavian models imported by the Vikings, probably crossed with Frisian or Saxon influences: long ships built with clinking and with curved and symmetrical extremities, adorned with sculpted prows (the angel on the *Mora*, armed with a spear and blowing the horn, is no less than a Christianised drek!), navigating by sail or by oar, and many of which are depicted on the Bayeux Tapestry. Furthermore, these characteristics appear to have been adopted over several centuries, as suggested by the clinked boat found in Fermanville, today dated back to the 13th or 14th century, but also in texts relating to "esneques" upon which Channel crossings were made within the Angevin Empire and whose name stems directly from the Viking Age *snekkja*, known to us thanks to the Ladby and Skuldelev 5 wrecks. This type of ship was particularly well adapted for transporting horses which, upon grounding, could climb over the gunwale without affecting the ship's balance: this is accurately depicted on the Bayeux Tapestry on the beach at Pevensey. Over and above these large carriers, William's fleet also included a number of small fishing-seagoing boats which are represented in smaller sizes. Wace therefore drew a distinction between "nefs" and "batels", the latter being devoid of a sculpted prow and having a boarding capacity of four or five men, but neither their horses nor their shields. However, rigging and steering rudders were common to all ships.

Within this antechamber of the Conquest of England, a motley crew was hard at work: that summer, seven thousand men camped around Dives, in Varaville or in the Cabourg dunes which formerly housed a small Roman fortress, built to drive out the Saxons. Its ruins, which stood at the top of a hillock overlooking the estuary, on the site of the former Vieux-Cabourg, were later accompanied by cabins used by

11th century Norman combatants, re-enactment near Battle Abbey.

the River Dives' fishermen-whalers, referred to as "Walmans", to store their harpoons, nets and small fishing boats. In this summer of 1066, the Cabourg camp was so vast that it later led to the foundation of a new parish devoted to Saint Michael, who vanquished over the dragon. It was home to dozens of large ecru-coloured tents to accommodate the combatants, who, by preference, were lodged outside villages. At night, it was advised to stay away from them. Ill-omened howls could be heard, along with screaming women, and brawls, which occasionally degenerated, were commonplace. However, by daytime, men were kept busy. The entire population flocked there, crossing the Dives to bring the troops their supplies and necessary equipment. Two men were needed to carry a hauberk, whilst dozens of carts transported foodstuffs and fodder, not forgetting the countless barrels of wine requested by the duke to treat his companions. Never before had the small port of Dives seen such commotion! The sound of hammers hitting red-hot iron could be heard all around the makeshift forges established on the outskirts of the port. The smoke of many a stove sent skywards smells of wood and of the bread, fish and meat needed to feed this ravenous army. It travelled miles, drifting on the wind that turned in time with the tide – all around, no-one was left unawares of what was happening here! The mocking cries of the seabirds intermingled with the dull clamours of the men as they called to each other or trained in combat across the dunes and the prairies. Thousands of untroubled horses grazed placidly, waiting for their hour, on the grassy strand. Some had been taken by boat to islets within the vast salty marsh. Every day, at low tide, dozens of grooms led them to the grounded ships for boarding. From a very early age, the Normans had accustomed these young horses to the sound of the horn, the clatter of weapons and the crashing of the sea. From time to time, a cavalcade led by some bear-headed lord, galloped to the sound of the horn, charging, one by one, against the training posts or setting off on a hunt in the Bavent woods. Rows of archers fired on straw targets as the squires relentlessly greased weapons, helmets and hauberks, to chase the rust

11th century Norman combatants, re-enactment near Battle Abbey.

that was rife in this salty sea air. When evening came, hundreds of campfires illuminated the Cabourg dunes. At nightfall, warmed with wine, daringly-worded songs resounded, scattered with the odd foreign accent. In the middle of the night, fights broke out, to be rapidly quelled by the duke's men.

On the 12th of August, the army was ready at last. Behind the shelter of the earthen walls of their small cottages, the people of Dives were eager to see the end of these turbulent and battle-thirsty neighbours. Then began a long wait for the 4,500 foot soldiers and 2,500 horsemen, who were gathered together on the banks of the estuary. For William was keen to take Harold by surprise, despite the immense army the latter had reunited on the opposite shore, around the Isle of Wight. And the Norman was oblivious to none of the ongoing preparations by his rivals, be they Saxons or Norwegians... Hence, although the Norman historian William of Jumièges, a contemporary of the event, explains that the Normans' long wait was due to unfavourable winds, perhaps we should consider an alternative explanation: that of William's cunning, for he was waiting for the perfect moment, in particular the equinoctial tides, whilst keeping his enemy standing at the ready as long as possible, to weaken and to irritate it. We know that throughout his life, William adopted a somewhat unconventional approach to war, undoubtedly partly inspired by the manners of his Viking ancestors... In 1066, William was extraordinarily well-informed by the spies he had despatched to all four corners of England, Flanders and perhaps even Norway. He knew that Tostig had schemed with Harald Hardraada. The previous spring, Tostig, who had taken the precaution of travelling to Normandy to elude his brother, set sail from Barfleur to the Isle of Wight, then "played Vikings" for a while on the south coast of England before heading for York. That was where Harold's loyal troops crushed Tostig's, forcing him to flee to Scotland. Meanwhile, Harald awaited his hour, ready to make battle. On the 12th of September, William was apparently informed of the imminent Norwegian attack. He then ordered for his fleet to head for Saint-Valery-sur-Somme, in the Ponthieu region, in order to position it directly opposite Pevensey, in Sussex, where the English Channel is narrower. He had the site adapted, in the utmost secret, to best accommodate his army on the grounds around Fécamp Abbey priory. The equinoctial tide saw the fleet leave Dives-sur-Mer to head towards the Somme estuary. On its long journey along the coast, the fleet suffered a few ship-wrecks; however, it finally reached Saint-Valery with relatively minor losses. Then began a new wait for the Normans, as they prayed the patron saint of sailors...

Monument in commemoration of the Battle of Stamford Bridge.

Less than a week later, on the 18th of September, Harald and Tostig's fleets joined forces in the Humber estuary, then their armies marched towards York. Harold was to speed his way up to northern England to challenge them. On the 20th, before Harold had arrived, the first battle took place in Fulford, two miles to the south of York. Harald won a crushing victory that opened the gates of York. Harold and his 6,000 men only reached York on the 24th. They nevertheless succeeded in taking the Norwegians by surprise the following day, on Stamford bridge. In the evening, after a day's carnage, Harald's men were chopped into pieces by the terrifying Danish axes brandished by Harold's elite warriors, referred to as *Housecarls*. Harald and Tostig's bodies were left on the battlefield and only twenty ships headed back to Norway, sounding the knell of the Viking era's great Scandinavian expeditions...

Meanwhile, William had set sail once more on the night of the 27th to the 28th. He was aware that part of Harold's army was posted in London and that his fleet was at Sandwich. He absolutely needed to prevent these two considerable armies from joining forces. Speed was also

of the essence for, once landed, there would be no way back for the Normans. The crossing was made by the light of the moon and the lanterns that lit the masts of the lead ships. The *Mora* was the first to land and William awaited the rest of his fleet. At dawn, in Pevensey, a thousand ships unloaded men, weapons and horses; William threw himself to the ground, then stood up, his hands full of sand, and cried to his troops, "By the glory of God, I hold the English soil in my two hands!". The experienced seamen berthed and freed the horses, as the pilots stabilised the boats with their poles. The boats were then dragged onto the beach, their masts lowered and their spars and rigging dismantled. The Normans moved inland towards Hastings, where Harold and his vanguard lay in wait.

Map of troop movements in 1066.

In red: Harold Godwinson.
In blue: Tostig Godwinson.
In yellow: William the Bastard.
In green: Harald Hardraada.

What followed went down in history: tales of the Battle of Hastings have spurred countless remarks that would be far too long to list here. After crushing the Norwegians at Stamford Bridge, then rushing back south to London, Harold marched to challenge William with but a fraction of his armed forces. This was precisely what the Norman had hoped for since, with his back to the sea, he had no choice but to win a fast and decisive victory. As tradition would have it, he even proposed a duel, which Harold refused... Based on reports by the historian Gui d'Amiens and scenes from the Bayeux Tapestry, Pierre Bouet offers a detailed account of the different phases of the battle. William's army comprised horsemen, foot soldiers and archers from across the Norman territory and those of its allies: Brittany, Le Mans, Flanders, along with horsemen and mercenaries from Sicily and southern Italy. On the evening of the 13th, Harold, accompanied by his brothers Gyrth and Leofwine, decided to wait no longer and to take action, in order to take the Normans by surprise. They took up position on the banks of Senlac Hill, which overlooks the prairie where the Normans were soon to gather. The battle began at dawn on the 14th of October.

On the evening of that terrible day, while the outcome was as yet unsure, the Normans engaged an ultimate manoeuvre, breaking through the English rampart and harassing the *Housecarls* who bitterly defended Harold and his brothers. William, with support from Eustace of Boulogne, Hugh of Ponthieu and one of the Giffard sons, set upon Harold who was killed by their blows, along with his brothers. The English then began to flee, abandoning the bodies of Godwin's sons and their red and white dragon standards...

The Battle of Hastings. Painting by François-Hippolyte Debon, 1844. Museum of Fine Arts, Caen, M. Seyve photographer.

The Viking Legacy

The Conquest of England by William the Conqueror is one of the most extraordinary episodes in European medieval history. A large number of publications, learned articles, comic strips, films and documentaries have focused on the event, whilst major commemorations are organised every year, not only in the meadow overlooked by Battle Abbey, in England, but also in Normandy, in Rouen, Bayeux, Caen, Falaise and Dives-sur-Mer... This famous crossing, which has already caused much ink to flow, continues to arouse great interest to this very day, not only in Normandy, but across a large part of the globe. The event was, of course, a rather atypical military

Re-enactment of the Battle of Hastings.

feat that its contemporaries most likely experienced as such. Let's recall what the chroniclers had to say about William's need to overcome the great reluctance demonstrated by many of his barons to engage in such a hazardous venture. Transporting such an army by sea, around a thousand years ago, was quite a challenge. Just think of the horses that needed to be embarked, then disembarked on the beach in Pevensey. Imagine the weight and the quantity of the weapons, food supplies and timber that William's companions had to transport on these sailing ships. And let us not forget the many men who died by drowning on the way to Saint-Valery-sur-Somme, before even beginning the true crossing...

Battle Abbey: stele in memory of Harold Godwinson.

The exceptional scale of the venture explains why this expedition was presented as a genuine miracle. Indeed, let us bear in mind that medieval historians were clerics, steeped in Latin and biblical culture. It is within this context that William of Normandy was represented almost like Moses, capable – thanks to divine intervention – of opening the tumultuous waters of the English Channel before his troops. Harold in turn was depicted as disloyal to God, after the oath he made over holy relics in Bayeux Cathedral to respect William's right to the English throne. This, indeed, is the main subject of the Bayeux Tapestry: to tell the tale of how William, led by his rightful legacy, was victorious over his rival who showed disloyalty to God. We already know that William the Conqueror was a pious man. As early as the 1040s, he obtained the benevolence of the Church by establishing God's peace throughout the duchy and by founding and bestowing rich monasteries, including St. Martin's in Troarn, and St. Stephen's and the Holy Trinity in Caen. These pious acts enabled him, in 1066, to receive benediction from the Pope who had the Papal Standard sent to him from Rome. Let's not forget the role attributed to intercessor saints, patrons of the churches under whose shadow the ships set sail: Notre Dame in Dives and Saint Valéry in Somme. Over and over again, 11th century texts remind us how eager William was to honour the saints in order to obtain their protection.

A thousand years later, the images associated with this event have obviously changed. The marvels and piousness of Christianity, to which medieval men looked at the time, have been gradually replaced by admiration for the courage of these conquerors, and, of course, insatiable curiosity as to their skills, their knowledge of the sea and of horses, and their capacity to brave the forces of nature to achieve their aims. Furthermore, the event began in Normandy and this 1066 crossing inevitably brings us to consider another, more recent and memorable landing operation: that of the 6th of June 1944. These major episodes in our history are bound, despite the centuries between them, by their common triple dimension – maritime, warfaring and international. In the collective memory, both events spur imagination and a thirst for knowledge, a quest for shared identity and heritage for those who live on both shores of the English Channel. They also both contribute towards large-scale cultural tourism, today recognised by all as one of Normandy's most striking assets. Given such widely renowned importance, the year 2016, which marks the 950th anniversary of the Conquest of England, will be celebrated in the towns bordering the Dives. Five years have gone by since the 1100th anniversary of the founding of Normandy by Rollo, a Viking chief of Norwegian origin and the direct ascendant of the dukes and the royal Anglo-Norman dynasty. On that occasion, an earlier book was published, focusing on what went on behind the scenes of the conquest, via historic and archaeological sources offering a contrast between preparations for the conquest and the local history of the Dives lower valley. The dual aim of the project was to enable visitors to Dives-sur-Mer to discover or to better under-stand these sites and their historic dimension, via a small reference work, conveniently sized yet as comprehensive as possible, reuniting available sources and archives.

Five years later, this new book approaches a question that, to date, has barely been covered in publications intended for the general public: why is the 1066 Channel crossing currently considered by European historians as the last great event of the Viking era in Western Europe and what does that interpretation mean? In an attempt to answer this question, we must place the Norman Conquest of England in a much larger context: that of the story of the Vikings and of their foundations, of which William's Normandy was a part. This story takes us a long way back in time, three centuries to be precise, to the beginnings of what is commonly referred to as the "Viking Age". Also, and first and foremost, we must define exactly what we mean by "Viking".

William the Conqueror Fairs in Dives-sur-Mer, 2016.

The Viking Age

Historians have agreed on an official beginning to the Viking Age, as it is generally accepted that the discovery of America by Christopher Columbus, in 1492, marked the end of the Middle Ages and the start of the early modern period. It is essentially a convenient landmark - a historic milestone we can use to consider the notion of a before and an after. This official Viking Age therefore began on the 8th of June 793, when pillagers from Norway, aboard long ships adorned with dragon heads, landed on the east coast of England and ravaged the monastery of Lindisfarne, founded a century earlier by Irish monks. This event, that the great English historian Saint Bede the Venerable relates in his famous *Anglo-Saxon Chronicle*, plunged the entire Christian world into terror. Death and desolation had come from the sea. The Lindisfarne monks first noticed a few sails on the horizon, before seeing a handful of ships land on the shore, their prows adorned with striking sculpted dragon heads. The ruffians that surged out of them immediately thrust upon the monastery, ransacking the church's treasures, murdering monks and peasants as they tried to flee in all directions, then setting fire to the buildings located inside the monastery enclosure, before heading back to their ships, laden with spoils, livestock and the poor slaves they had captured. When the sea engulfed them once more, all was ravaged, the hitherto peaceful monastery was in flames and the escapees mourned their lost ones before the smoking ruins of their wrecked huts...

Lindisfarne abbey.

The first English historian, hunted by the Vikings!

Saint Bede the Venerable was an Anglo-Saxon monk who gained fame after composing *The Ecclesiastical History of the English People,* a literary monument that is no less than the very first national historic source ever written in Great Britain. Very probably of noble origin, his birth is dated in 672 or 673 near Jarrow, in Northumbria, in northeast England. At the age of 7, he entered Wearmouth monastery, where he received religious instruction from its founder, Abbot Benedict Biscop. He then settled in Jarrow, a neighbouring community to Wearmouth, upon or shortly after its foundation in 682. Bede demonstrated extraordinary intellectual qualities. In just a few years, he became a learned man, a teacher and a writer, renowned throughout Great Britain. Upon his death on the 26th of May 735, he was buried in Jarrow. However, according to traditional belief, in the 11th century his remains were transported to Durham Cathedral where he is believed to rest to this very day.

Saint Bede the Venerable. Walters Art Museum de Baltimore, ms W148, fol. 3v.

The traumatised Lindisfarne monks then fled to Durham, in the county of Northumbria, in the very north of England. With them, they took their precious illuminated Gospels and the shrine containing the relics of St. Cuthbert, miraculously saved from the pillagers. Over the years that followed, dozens of monasteries met with the same fate, both in the British Isles and over the Continent. For the Vikings took the habit of coming back every spring, lured by the riches of the West, sailing up rivers and putting town and country to fire and sword. In 794, they attacked another monastic community, neighbour and daughter to Lindisfarne: Jarrow, of which Saint Bede the Venerable was a member. Then, in 795, their target was the sanctuary of Iona, in the Inner Hebrides, in northwest Scotland. Once more, it was a terrible shock, for this monastery, founded in 563 by St. Columba, the father of the Celtic churches of Ireland and Scotland, was considered as a highly symbolic Christian site. Hence, throughout the Western world, the Vikings were thought to be sent by the devil himself, all the more so when, as related in the Annals of Ulster, they ravaged Iona again in 802 and 806, murdering sixty-eight monks. The following year, the community deserted the Holy Isle to head for a new monastery built in Kells, located inland from Dublin.

Iona abbey.

Berserk on the Torslunda plaque.
Stockholm Museum of National
Antiquities.

The Viking terror was to continue till the early 900s. Accounts by medieval historians, the clerics that were as numerous as the terrorised monks, described them as bloodthirsty pagans whose name history has chosen to forget, sent by Satan to ravage the world. Let's be perfectly clear, once and for all: this portrait is not entirely false, for the wave of extreme violence spurred by the Vikings was undeniably true. Its major drawback lies, on the one hand, in the fact that it is incomplete, and in its insufficiency to explain all the whys and wherefores of the phenomenon. As violent as they may have been, these ferocious Vikings were men like any others and did not necessarily demonstrate greater violence than their Frankish, Anglo-Saxon or even American Indian contemporaries... It remains that the descriptions left by Western monks have found an echo over the centuries, in certain imaginary portraits offered by the authors of sagas, in particular the terrifying Berserks, those improbable characters in the form of invincible warrior-sorcerers who knew neither fear nor pity – bearded, hirsute individuals donning bear and wolf skins, covered with tattoos and scars and, of course, heavily laden with weapons... Once more, it would appear that reality has been somewhat deformed under the fantastic features of the typical Berserk. We know that certain Viking communities survived exclusively from the profession of arms, working as mercenaries for the highest bidder, whilst nevertheless abiding by a highly specific and most probably partly religious code of honour. The decapitated bodies of fifty of these "beast warriors", whose name is believed to depict the way they "fought like bears", i.e. naked or without armour, may well have been unearthed by English archaeologists in Weymouth, in the county of Dorset. To frighten their enemies, some of these elite combatants filed their teeth. This is all quite mysterious. Whatever the truth, this motley portrait for a long time prevailed in historic studies on the Vikings, to become a universal image, which we still find to this day, solidly established in advertising, trade, literature and cinema. Also, in order to be fully grasped, the word "Viking" requires prior explanation, for the character it depicts has been tainted with so many clichés produced by our own imaginations since the Middle Ages.

The Riðgway Hill Viking burial pit

Ridgeway Hill Viking burial pit, Weymouth: overall view of the excavation site. Excavation by Oxford Archaeology.

The Ridgeway Hill Viking burial pit, located near Weymouth in Dorset, was discovered in 2009 by a team of English archaeologists (Oxford Archaeology). It contains 54 decapitated and dismembered skeletons and 51 skulls belonging to men, the majority of whom were aged under 30, who died according to radio-carbon dating between 910 and 1030. They were all killed at the same time by means of a sharp weapon, such as a sword. Many received multiple blows to the vertebrae, jawbone and skull. The absence of any clothing appears to suggest they were stripped naked before being killed. Their bones, skulls, rib cages and lower limbs were placed in separate piles in a former quarry specifically used for the occasion and located on the outskirts of a former medieval parish. The missing skulls may have been kept to be exhibited.

Archaeologists believe this burial pit to be that of Vikings, executed by Anglo-Saxons after a battle. Isotopic analysis of teeth has offered confirmation of their Scandinavian origin, with the exception of one man, originating from the Arctic region. The circumstances of the massacre are unknown, yet it bears witness to the violent events that reigned throughout the Anglo-Saxon world during the great 10th century Viking invasions.

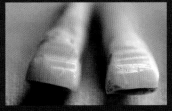

Filed teeth found in Weymouth.

The Viking, an unfamiliar figure

At the beginning of the Viking Age, these men that the Anglo-Saxons referred to as "Northmen", later to become the French "Normans", were indeed from Scandinavia. Yet all Scandinavians were not Vikings and, likewise, all Vikings were not from Scandinavia as the phenomenon gradually reached other territories. They were a group of men whose definition did not lie in their origins (and even less in their genes, a concept which was of course totally unknown to medieval men!), but in a specific activity: that of seafaring expeditions to distant lands. That is precisely what the word "Viking" means in the Norse language that was common to ancient Scandinavian populations. It comes from the root "*vik*" which signifies a natural harbour within a bay or a cove. The "Viking" was consequently the "man of the *vik*", in other words, a coastal inhabitant, a man whose life focused on the sea and, by extension, on maritime expeditions of all sorts.

Yet, misunderstanding of this word and what it encompasses has led to many a caricature of Vikings! Of course, these men were neither timorous nor even necessarily pacifistic and the violence of their invasions is perfectly veracious. Yet, it would be extremely simplistic to imagine them exclusively as sanguinary warriors, for they were in fact sailors, fishermen and peasants, travellers and traders, capable of turning into pillagers should the opportunity present itself. Some of them earned their living from war, selling their services as mercenaries; there are many well-known examples in Normandy, even almost up to William's time. However, were these men so different from the many mercenaries and adventurers from Normandy, Brittany, Flanders and elsewhere, who comprised a vast share of the 1066 army?

The vik in the town of Vík, county of Sogn og Fjordane.

ikings on an illumination on the life of Saint
Ibinus of Angers.

We must get rid of another cliché: the caricature. First of all, let's establish once and for all that the Vikings were not all blond-haired giants, nor were they uneducated barbarians. If we refer to a famous example, the fact that, in the Middle Ages, all Scandinavians were not blond is clearly confirmed in the Icelandic sagas written a few centuries later by Snorri Sturluson. What can we say of the hero named Njall "the Burnt", i.e. the "basan", of black hair and dark skin, other than that he is of no liking, from a physical point of view, to the image of the blond giant that has been so widely spread? What's more, a long time before the Viking Age, these Northmen already abided by laws, were familiar with art and poetry, and shared social values. The most important of these values were courage and cunning, success and wealth which they attributed to the favours of their gods and the force of fate which, for them, governed all things throughout the universe. And it was precisely in order to acquire such prized qualities that many became Vikings and set off on adventure. The mark left by their passing bears witness to the various dimensions of their activity: pillaging, murder, fires on the one hand, but also the foundation of towns and trading posts, where goods, words and skills were exchanged.

The Viking expedition could in fact take on many different faces. It could be in the form of an exploratory journey aimed at discovering virgin territories and settling there. It could also be, when the opportunity arose, a trade-related journey, or a warfaring raid aimed at pillaging riches from foreigners or at kidnapping slaves. Whether they were exchanged or stolen, whether they were inanimate objects or human beings considered as simple merchandise, the goods and slaves brought back by the Vikings brought fortune to their new possessors. Such was the quest of the Northmen who set off to "play Vikings" overseas, risking their lives: simply to achieve prestige and wealth.

One last cliché needs to be sorted: that of the multitude of Vikings that came from Nordic lands to colonise Europe. This is probably the most false and the most deformed image that has ever been created concerning the Vikings, for their numbers were well below those likely to result in such large-scale colonisation! Around the year 800, there were very few Scandinavians, and consequently very few Vikings. They comprised a particular and select population, for it appears clear that not everyone could become a Viking. They were essentially young men, capable of travelling across the seas in quest of the wealth that would, upon their return, transform them into powerful and respected men. Such motivation, together with coping with the harshness of their daily lives, was not within everyone's reach! Some were exiled noblemen, others were merchants or mercenaries, but they were all looking for fortune, for which they paid the price, by taking great risks.

Snorri Sturluson (1179-1241)

Snorri Sturluson was an Icelandic writer famous for his sagas and mythological poems which comprise a major literary and historic contribution. The story of his life is related in the *Sturlunga Saga,* named after his father, Sturla, and compiled around 1300 by several anonymous writers. Snorri was born and bred in Hvammur in Iceland and was from one of the first colonised families of Norwegian origin. From his early childhood, he familiarised himself with Icelandic historic and mythological tradition, and, simultaneously, with the great Christian works.

Snorri Sturluson, by H. Stefanson, circa 1930.

As an adult, he assumed major political and diplomatic roles on behalf of the Kings of Norway, which did not prevent him from producing several brilliant, poetic and historic works, such as the heroic *Edda* series, the *Chronicle of the Kings of Norway* (*Heimskringla*) and other independent sagas such as the *Enigma of Egill,* today considered as literary monuments. In the 13th century, increasing tension between Norway and Iceland placed Snorri in an extremely difficult position given the hatred he inspired among several Icelandic clan leaders, along with the king's mistrust of a man who had always remained faithful to his island. In the autumn of 1241, King Håkon IV the Old (1204-1263) commanded a murderous raid against the Snorri home in Reykholt, having Snorri spinelessly assassinated.

A page from *Snorri's Edda*, an 18th century Icelandic manuscript.

The Vikings, migrants that made history

The Vikings were a handful of adventurers who set off to conquer the world. Many never returned, either settling overseas or, and probably more frequently, losing their lives.

It is a well-known fact that historians and archaeologists have very little accurate information on their precise numbers. The rare figures mentioned in chronicles left by medieval historians, excavation in major Scandinavian burial grounds and the overseas towns where they settled, along with supposed Viking sepulchres discovered across the British Isles or on the Continent (where they are a far rarer phenomenon), have enabled us to deduce that a few tens of thousands of Northmen effectively settled in the immense territory covered by the Viking expeditions. As such, the number of migrants never surpassed the native populations with which they mixed, sometimes very quickly, as was the case in Normandy.

'Sur la trace des Vikings'. Sculpture by Georges Saulterre, 1990, erected alongside the A13 Paris-Normandy motorway in memory of the Vikings.

We must also consider the time and the pace of their settlement. The Viking Age spread over three successive phases, during which Scandinavian migration changed considerably. In the early period, from 790 to around 850, their aim was to leave their homeland temporarily, then to return there with the spoils gathered during the expedition. Then, little by little, this early phase, referred to as the "Viking raids", gave way to a second phase which mobilised more men and, more specifically, warriors. Henceforth committed to pillaging and conquering new territories with genuine armies, commanded by great chiefs, the phase stretched from around 850 to the early 900s. It was precisely at the end of this second Viking wave, referred to as the "Scandinavian foundations", that early Normandy was founded in 911.

Then, till the late 10th century, the Viking Age experienced a third phase of development involving settlement and political establishment. The territories conquered by the Vikings covered an immense perimeter, stretching from Greenland to Western Russia. The fourth and last phase then continued up to the mid 11th century. It came to an end, in Normandy, with the Conquest of England and the advent of an Anglo-Norman state that was to survive till 1204. It was the period of great kingdoms and dynasties of Viking origin, which emerged from the Channel basin to Western Russia. To the west, beyond the British Isles, the Vikings founded other sustainable settlements in Iceland, along with trading posts on the coast of Greenland, Canada and North America, five centuries before Christopher Columbus! Eastwards, the Swedes crossed the Baltic Sea as far as the Slavic lands which became the cradle of present-day Russia. From the region around Saint Petersburg and the city of Kiev, they sailed down the great Russian rivers as far as Byzantium, on the banks of the Black Sea, to reach the gates of the Muslim Middle East.

Hence, in two centuries, the Vikings sailed all the known seas in the world, even pushing the limits of contemporary knowledge as far as the American continent! From a historical point of view, this Viking adventure marked one of the major phases of the opening up of the Western world, the following phase being the great 15th century Portuguese and Spanish explorers, before James Cook and the conquest of space. This is why their foundations, such as those in Normandy and Kievan Rus', were already integrated within a large-scale international cultural and political context. This is also why, in 1066, as he took to the seas with a thousand dragon-headed ships, William the Conqueror acted as the perfect heir to his Viking ancestors. Just as they had, he set off on an adventure across unsure seas and with no guarantee of return. The immense territory he had reunited by the end of his life gave way to a new Anglo-Norman state, stretching across both shores: the Plantagenets, whose political decomposition in 1204 was nevertheless pursued by an ultimate momentum during the Hundred Years' War.

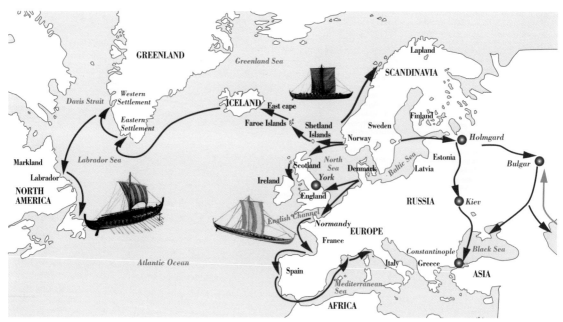

World map of the Viking expeditions.

The origins of the Viking Age, the "Germanic seafarers"

The Vikings came from Scandinavia, in other words from the Northern European countries that are today referred to as Norway, Sweden and Denmark. Finland was, at the time, inhabited by Laplanders, a distinct population from that of the remaining vast share of Scandinavia. In these lands, the climate was far colder than elsewhere in Europe. Furthermore, although Scandinavia offers extremely varying landscapes, including high mountain ranges, fertile valleys, immense forests, numerous lakes, marshes and large coastal plains, but also deep sea lakes, referred to as fjords, life there was particularly difficult in medieval times. The climate was of great importance for the agricultural economy. The Atlantic coast, to the west, is milder and, as one travels eastwards, the climate becomes colder and winters are harsh. Light varies according to the seasons, the north being plunged into the darkness of polar night throughout the winter. Very early, the natural environment spurred the Scandinavian people to adopt a lifestyle adapted to winter conditions and to count on the nourishing resources offered by the sea. A vast share of the population was established in southern Scandinavia, along the coast, living from agriculture and fishing, metalworking and tree farming in the immense forests.

At the start of the Viking Age, the frontiers of the land were unclear; they changed depending on the game of influences and alliances between the former people of the North, who, far from federated in the form of nations, were ruled over by several kings and a multitude of chiefs who fought over power. Yet, they all spoke the same language - Old Norse - and, as Germanic people, they shared the same ethnic and cultural origin. Indeed, just like the Franks, the Saxons, the Frisians, the Angles and the Jutes, the Scandinavians were Germanic people "from the West", who had travelled to central Europe during the prehistoric period. Although these different populations had distinct histories, they were nevertheless reunited by a shared linguistic, cultural and religious base, and they travelled, during ancient times, to the same vast geographical region: the Channel basin and the North Sea. These Northmen, who settled along the coast, very quickly learned to live in time with the sea. They all knew how to build great boats capable of sailing from port to port, from fjord to fjord or from island to island, to fish, to trade, to transport or to wage war. So, at the very start of the Viking Age, the Scandinavians had already, for centuries over, challenged the North Sea and the Baltic basins. Due to winter freezing and the difficulty of travelling inland, coastal and sea navigation were the safest and the fastest ways to connect people.

Yet, in the 500-550s, the populations in these northern regions increased, leading to a series of migrations to the northwest of the European continent and to the southeast of the British Isles. In Scandinavia, the vast necropolises excavated by archaeologists in Vendel and Valsgärde, on the eastern coast of Sweden, bear witness to major changes in society. Several graves house the remains of armed men, buried with great care by their peers to ensure they may continue to travel in the beyond. Over and above their weapons, shields, spears, swords and impressively

The Venðel cemetery

Helmet from the Vendel cemetery, 7th century. Stockholm Museum of National Antiquities.

The Vendel cemetery is located in the province of Uppland, in Sweden, in the vicinity of a former palace where the first Swedish kings took up residence. Discovered in 1881 by the Swedish archaeologist Hjalmar Stolpe, it is home to a group of large burial mounds containing an entire, ten metre-long ship, used for its owner's last journey. The mark of the clinking has remained fossilised in the surrounding earth, whilst the iron rivets used to hold it in place were found during excavation. The funerary furnishings that adorned these sepulchres are both rich and varied, occasionally comprised of genuine treasures. Certain objects, particularly worthy of note, include weapons, among which richly ornate dress swords and helmets adorned with stylised animal decors, shields, but also cauldrons, jewellery, tools, etc. All these objects date from the 5th to the 8th century. Today, the helmets are particularly famous. They are similar to those found in the extraordinary royal cemetery in Sutton Hoo, in southeast England, which may be the last resting place of the great Anglo-Saxon King Rædwald of East Anglia (circa 599-624), buried in a twenty-seven metre-long ship! The relationship between these vast Scandinavian and Anglo-Saxon cemeteries also gives evidence of a cultural community between these different populations who, at the time, shared the northern maritime basins. Many animal sacrifices have also been identified at Vendel; most of them horses, which were symbols of wealth and warfaring virtue. The men buried in these great cemeteries were undoubtedly particularly rich and prominent figures thanks to their maritime expeditions. The exceptional nature of this cemetery has led Scandinavian historians to date it to the period that preceded the Viking Age, still considered in Nordic countries as belonging to the Iron Age (in France, the end of the Iron Age coincided with the Gallic period and with the Roman Conquest, half a century BC).

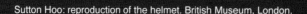

Sutton Hoo: reproduction of the helmet. British Museum, London.

adorned helmets, many precious objects were also buried with them, illustrating the great wealth associated with an economy built on exchange and on warfare. Slaves and symbolic animals were also sacrificed during funerals. These graves were formed of a burial mound in the shape of a boat's hull and surrounded with raised stones. The whole was evocative of a great ship upon which, based on their beliefs, ancient Scandinavians believed the deceased would travel to the beyond.

And the North was transformed

During the Viking era, the Scandinavian countries we know today were not yet formed and Scandinavia was shared between several kingdoms and principalities held by independent peoples who, depending on successive alliances, lived in peace or at war. The spoils brought back from Viking expeditions enabled some to impose themselves by force, yet unity was a gradual process and only resulted in the emergence of the first great Scandinavian kingdoms during the 10th century. The same applied in the rest of the Western world, in Great Britain in particular. In the early 600s, England was divided into a dozen small Anglo-Saxon kingdoms, the three most important of which were Northumbria in the north, Mercia in the centre and Wessex in the south-west. Ireland and Scotland were divided into kingdoms of distinct civilisations which shared power. It was within this context that the Vikings appeared in 793; in just a few years, failing the encounter with any genuine resistance, they succeeded in establishing themselves in many locations across the British Isles.

Things were more complicated on the Continent. In the north, the Vikings were to confront the military power of the Frankish world, governed by Charlemagne and his Carolingian heirs. The Saxons and, in particular, the Frisians, who controlled the ports of Hamburg and Dorestad, which welcomed the vast majority of sea traffic between the North Sea and the Baltic Sea, became their subjects. It was only in the year 911, after decades of raids that mobilised increasing numbers of troops, that Rollo managed to settle on the banks of the Seine. Yet he did not do so as a conqueror, but as a subject of the Frankish king. The Northmen settled as early as the late 9th century in various locations throughout present-day France, via a process that, despite what may have been said of it, bore no comparison to a planned and massive colonisation. Such a movement by the Scandinavian people is simply unthinkable for, around the year 900, they were no more unified than the British were.

The formation of Scandinavian kingdoms was a gradual phenomenon at the time, only to become solidly established at the beginning of the year 1000, with the emergence of the great royal dynasties and the Christianisation of Scandinavia. The Vikings unconsciously played a major role in this evolution. Through the Vikings, colossal riches were displaced across the northern European maritime routes, to flood the major trading ports of Scandinavia. These riches were in the form of tonnes of coins which the Vikings, who only became familiar with currency in the 11th century, melted down to transform them into ingots and heavy bracelets which were kept as treasures. They also included tonnes of precious goods, brought back from the four corners of the globe over their travels: amber and fur from the Baltic region, honey and wax from the forests of Russia, perfume and silk from the East, ivory and fur from the Great North, damascened weapons from the Frankish Empire... They also brought back slaves, a genuine human livestock rounded up wherever the Vikings passed.

In the early Viking Age, Sweden was shared by three civilisations: the Geats in the southwest, the Swedes in the east and the Gutes on the island of Gotland, in the middle of the Baltic Sea. The Swedes (*Suiones* in Latin) were the most powerful. In particular, they controlled the large town of Birka, located on the banks of Lake Mälaren, upstream of Stockholm, on the east coast of Sweden. During the Viking Age, Birka was a major and highly active trading port. As early as the 7th century, the Swedes and the Gutes from Gotland had sailed across the Baltic Sea and the North Sea, trading with distant lands, from Friesland to the Middle East, accumulating immense riches in the process. Around 970, these populations were finally reunited under the banner of the same king, Eric the Victorious (*Segersäll,* 945-994 or 995), who, succeeding a long line of semi-legendary chiefs, is said to have established his power as far as the nearby kingdom of Denmark.

In Denmark, around 730, the Danes joined forces to build an immense rampart aimed at protecting them from the Franks who threatened from the south: the Danevirke. It was in fact a huge, seven metre-high earthen embankment, surrounded by a wooden stockade and further protected by a ditch. Over a distance of thirty kilometres, it can still be seen today, thirteen centuries later. It forms a barrier from one extremity to the other of the Jutland peninsula, in the Schleswig-Holstein region, hence separating Denmark from the land of the Saxons, which was part of Charlemagne's empire. This large bor-der fortification, which was raised several times throughout the Middle Ages, was an efficient means of defence for the Danes. Around the year 800, their king, Godfred (before 804-810), rich from the Viking expeditions, was sufficiently powerful to dare to defy the King of the Franks, Charlemagne. In 810, he sent a fleet of two hundred ships to Friesland to ravage the vast port of Dorestad, at the mouth of the Rhine, and to take control of the maritime routes between the Channel and the North Sea. He succeeded; however, he died the same year, assassinated by his nephew Hemming, who later colluded with Charlemagne. Over later years, the Franks regularly intervened in Danish affairs whilst Denmark was progressively Christianised. Nevertheless, in 813, Horik, one of Godfred's sons, acceded to the throne. In the 830s, he resumed the Viking raids against the Frisians, ravaging their major port in Dorestad several times. Then, during the 840s, it was the Frankish

The Danevirke rampart.

coasts' turn: Paris was besieged in 845 by the legendary Viking Ragnar Shaggy Breeches (*Lodbrók, ?* – circa 850), whilst Horik in person sailed up the Elbe ahead of a fleet of six hundred ships and devastated Hamburg. Then Bordeaux and Périgueux fell in 848 and 849, intense raids continuing over the following decades, both in the North Sea and on both shores of the Channel, whilst the Danish sovereigns unified their kingdom and gave new momentum to Christianity. Between the late years of the 9th and the first decade of the 10th century, the crown was confiscated for a while by a Swedish lineage. Then the Danes, Harthacanute and his son Gorm the Old managed to reclaim the throne. Gorm the Old, who reigned from 936 to 958, gained fame for, among other feats, having had a runestone erected in memory of his wife, Thyra Danebod, in front of his palace in Jelling where his body was very probably unearthed in 1978. Yet, in his *Gesta Danorum*, (the Deeds of the Danes) composed around 1200, the great historian Saxo Grammaticus, presents her as the daughter of the King of England (perhaps Æthelstan, circa 894-939, who died with no male heirs), hence inaugurating a long and shared history between the two crowns... Their daughter, Gunnor, later married one of the first barons of Normandy, Ranulf de Crépon, who was no less than the ancestor of the famous Seneschal Osbern, assassinated as he tried to protect the young Duke William in 1040 at the Château du Vaudreuil.

Norway in turn remained for a long time divided into a dozen small feudal principalities in the hands of independent lords, referred to as jarls. The rivalry between them was extremely bitter. Around 880, after many a battle, one of them – Harald Fairhair (*Hárfagri*, circa 850-933), finally led his fleet to crush his rivals. In doing so, he became the first King of Norway, reigning in particular over the richest territories located in the south of the country. The life of the first great Norwegian king is related, in particular, via sagas in his honour – semi-legendary accounts written in the 12th century, a long time after his death. At the age of just 10, he is said to have succeeded his father in control of a principality located in southeast Norway. According to legend, his nickname comes from an oath he made to never cut or comb his hair before having reunited all the kingdoms of Norway under his sole control. One thing is certain - in the 860s, he set off on a series of expeditions and conquests throughout the neighbouring principalities. His authority gradually spread, by means of force, until a decisive battle against his rivals in Hafr fjord, which he won. There is an account of the battle in the *Chronicle of the Kings of Norway* by Snorri Sturluson, which also mentions, among others,

Representation of Dorestad by J.-C. Golvin. Arles Museum of Antiquity.

arald Fairhair and his father, Halfdan the Black. Illumination
om the Icelandic manuscript *Flateyjarbók*. Árni Magnússon
stitute, Reykjavík, GKS 1005 fol., late 14th century.

the great battle that opposed the Norwegians and Harold's troops at Stamford Bridge in 1066. Harald Fairhair's reign was far from a restful one. In 931, one evening, preceded by incessant skirmishes against his rivals, he handed over his crown to his son, Eric Bloodaxe (*Blodøks*, circa 885-954), a fearsome Viking who, faithful to his epithet, did not hesitate to have his seventeen brothers decapitated! Only one escaped: Håkon the Good (*den Gode*, circa 920-961), who was placed under the protection of King Æthelstan (circa 894-939), the first great sovereign of unified England. Two years later, upon their father's death, Håkon sailed to Norway with a fleet armed by his protector, succeeding in driving out his brother who then left to play Vikings in the British Isles...

The first Nordic towns

Each of the three emerging Scandinavian kingdoms saw the development of a few major port and trading centres, offering those in control of them immense financial resources. Birka in Sweden, Ribe and Hedeby/Haithabu in Denmark and in the north of present-day Germany, and Kaupang in Norway were among the first towns in Scandinavian history. Although, for many, their foundation dates back to the period of Frisian seafaring supremacy, their development, as from the year 800, was closely linked with Viking trade.

Birka is located on an island in the great Lake Mälaren in Sweden, around thirty kilometres to the west of Stockholm. Its history is known in particular thanks to archaeological excavation undertaken after the 1870s. Only a few Frankish sources make reference to the town and there is no written evidence emanating from Scandinavia itself. The very name, Birka, is a Latinised form, probably derived from the word *birk*, signifying a marketplace. We know that Birka was founded around 750 and that its trading peak was between 800 and 950 thanks to its port and to Viking expeditions led by Swedes across the Baltic region and as far as Russia and the Middle East.

The port of Birka was a grounding site offering comprehensive timber-built facilities and equipment, including pontoons and rudimentary lodgings for merchants. Craftsmen and travellers from distant lands stayed there and archaeologists have found many treasures including Arabic, English, Frankish and Byzantine coins. The Birka merchants exchanged local produce, amber from the Baltic region, fur and deer antlers, iron, together with expensive importations such as silver in all its forms, glassware, silk, spices, luxury crockery and also slaves, essentially of Slavic origin.

Map of the Scandinavian Viking towns.

Birka was brutally abandoned around 960, for the nearby town of Sigtuna, designated as the capital by the Kings of Sweden, and for the island of Gotland where an incredible quantity of Arabic coins was found – dirhams, a quantity almost equivalent to the accumulated total ever found elsewhere across the globe. The increasing scarcity of silver due to the exhaustion of Arabian mines in the late 10th century is one of the explanations for this sudden exclusion. In 1933, Birka was listed as a UNESCO world heritage site.

Today, Hedeby (Haithabu in modern German) is located in the far north of Germany, in the province of Schleswig-Holstein, at the base of the Jutland peninsula. During the Viking Age, it was part of the Danish territory. The site, which is linked to the Baltic Sea and the North Sea via two internal rivers, reached its peak thanks to its port and to Viking expeditions between the 8th and the 10th century. In light of archaeological excavation conducted since 1900, the town is considered as one of Denmark's oldest, along with Ribe, located to the west of Jutland. They were both founded in the 8th century, Ribe apparently first, then Hedeby around 770. The town's timber vestiges have been exceptionally preserved and, to date, investigations have only covered 5% of the town and 1% of the port.

Hedeby was mentioned for the very first time in a text dating from 804. At the time, King Godfred of Denmark launched expeditions against the Slavs and had the resulting spoils and slaves brought to the new town. He also had the Danevirke reinforced and, on the same occasion, the city walls were integrated within the great earthen rampart that closed off their Jutland peninsula. Hedeby owed its fortune to maritime trade between the Frankish world and Scandinavia, and to its ideal location between the North Sea and the Baltic Sea. Around 850, it became Denmark's leading marketplace. It welcomed travellers from across the globe, including Hispano-Arabic voyagers such as Ibrahim ibn Yaqub Al-Tartushi (Abraham ben Jacob) who left an astonishing description of the town. It would appear that the town minted its own coins, perhaps as early as the 10th century, which was quite exceptional in Scandinavia. The houses in Hedeby were tightly lined up and entirely made of timber. Planked pathways led to the port or formed jetties upon which boats could berth. Travelling merchants flocked there. Life was harsh due to the dampness and the cold caused by the marshes; diet was essentially based on fish. Yet, women were free to divorce, and Al-Tartushi also described their beauty and the custom for both men and women to wear make-up...

In 1050, the King of Norway, Harold "the Hard Ruler" (*Hardraada*, v. 1015-1066) had set fire to the town by sending several blazing ships into the harbour. Archaeologists have since found their wrecks in the Schlei fjord. Barely had it recovered from the disaster when Hedeby was ravaged and burnt once more by the Slavs in 1066. It never recovered.

Kaupang, whose name means "marketplace", is the first known conurbation in Norway. During the Viking Age, its name may have been Skiringssal. The town is located in Tjølling, near the modern-day town of Larvik, in the county of Vestfold. The market town, founded from nothing in the 780s, enjoyed intense trading favoured by the Viking raids until the mid 10th century. Its dry harbour was located on the beach of the Larvik fjord. Archaeological excavation conducted as from 1867 unearthed dense timber housing and a large cemetery to its north, along with the presence of several merchants and craftsmen, in particular blacksmiths and silversmiths, but also weavers, glassmakers and amber pearl or sharpening stone makers.

Around 900, Kaupang was home to around a thousand inhabitants. Local resources included iron, steatite (a soft stone used to make containers) and fish. However, Kaupang's fortune was first and foremost the result of Viking trade. Evidence is in the form of the few hundred thousand objects discovered in its inhabited areas among which Frankish and Arabic coins, other

gold coins from Dorestad, a thousand glass pearls imported from the banks of the Caspian Sea, the Black Sea and the Mediterranean, gold and bronze jewels, Frankish glassware, crockery from the Rhine, Denmark and the south coast of the Baltic Sea, weapons, tools, etc.

The site began a rapid decline between 950 and 970, before being abandoned and covered with forests and crops. This may have been caused by the diminution of Danish power in favour of the Kings of Norway.

Silver treasure found in Hägvalds. Gotland Museum, Visby, Sweden.

"Drakkars"

The early Viking Age coincided with maritime expansion beyond the Scandinavians' regional basin. This was made possible thanks to a major innovation in the nautical field: the introduction of sails, around the year 700. This innovation gave way to the design of the Viking ship, often referred to as the "drakkar" to which they greatly owed their renown. Today, it has been firmly established that this name, which was first used in French in the mid 19th century, was inspired by a Scandinavian word referring, not to their ships but to their sculpted prows, called *dreki*, representing fantastic animals, dragons or sea monsters. These sculpted heads were originally designed to terrify the protective divinities of enemy populations or of the Vikings' victims. For indeed, the Scandinavians, who only converted to Christianity in the 11th century, believed in a pantheon of gods, the most famous of whom were Odin and Thor, and in a great number

Sculpted bow and stem of the *Dreknor*, a reproduction of a Viking ship built on the occasion of the 'Tonnerres de Brest' maritime festival in 2012.

Ships with figureheads. Scene 38 from the Bayeux Tapestry.

of other divinities and fantastic creatures such as trolls and elves. It is quite striking to see the sculpted prows depicted on the Bayeux Tapestry, which are identical to the ones that adorned Viking ships in the 800s and 900s, particularly when considering that, during William's lifetime, Normandy was a Christian land. In all evidence, the Scandinavian tradition of sculpted prows withstood the test of time and of Christianisation, by preserving its warfaring symbolism: to spur courage and force among the Vikings, whilst discouraging their adversaries. This is why the Bayeux Tapestry continued to depict, in the period around 1070-1080, Scandinavian ships directly inspired by a naval concept elaborated during the Viking Age.

The first clinker-built boats

Before the Viking Age, Scandinavian boats, just like their Frisian and Anglo-Saxon neighbours, were exclusively oar-powered and consisted of a slender hull, built using the clinker technique and devoid of a keel, with a levelled base. Two wrecks of these longships have been studied by archaeologists and bear witness to their evolution: the ship found in Nydam, dated back to the first half of the 4th century, and the one in Sutton Hoo, dated to the early 7th century.

The great Nydam boat, 4th century. Engraving by F. Jung-Ilsenheim, Leipzig, 1937.

The Nydam ship is the largest of a group of three wrecks discovered in 1863 in Nydam Mose, a vast peaty lake located in Øster Sottrup in Denmark. It was sunk in the lake in perfect condition, most likely during a sacrificial ceremony, along with a second ship that had been entirely dismantled, and a third, also intact but made of pine. Only the largest ship, made of oak and powered by thirty rowers, has been kept in the Schleswig museum. Its timber, dated using dendrochronology, was from trees felled between 310 and 320, whereas it was sunk around 340-350. From 1989 to 1997, complementary excavation on the same site unveiled two 1.4 metre-long oak beams upon which bearded men's faces were sculpted, along with a pine rudder. Today, it is presumed that these stakes were attached to the boat's bow and used as mooring pegs. The Nydam boat is of great importance for it is the first known example of a clinker-built ship, i.e. with a hull made of long planks assembled horizontally in such a manner that their edges overlap, somewhat like tiles. This type of construction, which was an absolute novelty in the early 4th century, later became the very emblem of these Nordic longships, to remain so up to modern times. For example, up to the early 20th century, the technique was still used on certain traditional boats in Normandy, such as "caïques" from Yport-Étretat and "picoteux" from the Bay of Seine.

The Sutton Hoo boat was discovered in 1939 near Woodbridge in the county of Suffolk in England. It was dated to around 625 thanks to the treasure and the coins it transported. Its wooden features have totally disappeared; however, archaeologists found the mark left by the hull in the sediment round the burial mound. They also discovered iron rivets. The ship, which was driven by forty rowers, was 27 metres long and 4.2 metres wide. Just like the Nydam boat, it had neither a wide keel nor a sail. It was only between 650 and 700 that the Scandinavians truly adopted the use of the sail on longships. This was not because they were unaware of the concept, for small fishing boats in Nordic regions were already equipped with sails, but, first and foremost because

Excavation around the Sutton Hoo ship, 1939.

these longships were no longer destined exclusively for ceremonial use but for distant warfaring and trading expeditions. The introduction of a sail required a larger keel, to ensure the ship's stability under sail. The hull of these ships was deepened and a sectional view of it resembles a typographic brace (}) which became characteristic of Viking ships. Henceforth, the Northmen had at their disposal a genuine "machine fit for navigation" which enabled them to travel further and faster, to manoeuvre in the wind, to use the sail or the oars, to head up estuaries and to ground on shores or riverbanks. In the 8th century, they travelled further away from the coast towards the Baltic and the North Sea to head, two centuries later, for Russia and America! They were excellent sailors, using the stars, the moon and the currents as their guide, and always observing nature, shoals of cetaceans and seabirds. Their instinct was as extraordinary as their courage for many expeditions took them well beyond any guarantee of return, there where legends spoke of the ends of the earth, guarded by terrifying monsters.

The knowledge we now have of boats from the Viking Age relies not only on a number of representations engraved on steles, occasionally associated with runes, but in particular on the archaeology of wrecks, be they engulfed by the depths of the seas, deliberately sunk in a lake, such as the Nydam boat, or used as a sepulchre in the burial mound of an illustrious figure. Such information is complemented by descriptions given in sagas and by the scenes of the Bayeux Tapestry, even if they are less reliable since they date from a far more recent period than the Viking Age as such.

Ship burials from the Viking Age

Oseberg is undoubtedly the most famous of the ship burials dating from the Viking Age. It was discovered in 1904, under a burial mound located to the west of the Oslo fjord in Vestfold, in Norway. It was a large clinker-built ship, almost entirely made of oak and of a length of twenty-two metres and a beam of five metres. The wreck is now exhibited in the Viking Ship Museum in Oslo. Built around 820, this magnificently adorned ship was designed for short journeys, probably ceremonial outings for a high-ranking personality for whom it was later used for a ship burial. Its sculpted prow, considered as a master-piece of Viking art, has given its name to a particular ornamental style. Its ninety square metre sail, hoisted on a ten metre-long mast, enabled it to reach a speed of ten knots. Its crew was comprised of thirty oarsmen. Archaeologists also discovered a large steering rudder, an iron anchor and, more importantly, a formidable sepulchre containing the skeletons of two women, one aged between 60 and 70 years and the other around 50. Their funerary containers were dated by dendrochronology to the year 834, which led archaeologists and historians

The Oseberg ship, exhibited in the Viking Ship Museum in Oslo.

to suppose that the older of the two could have been the King of Norway Harald Fairhair's grandmother, named Åsa. Whatever their true identity, their remains are most probably those of two high-ranking women. They were buried along with a funerary treasure comprising a great number of superbly sculpted wooden objects including four sleighs, a small four-wheeled wooden cart, beds, chests and a sumptuous wardrobe including garments made of wool and Asian silk, and tapestries. The absence of any metal indicates that the grave was partly emptied by pillagers before it was discovered.

Archaeological excavation in Oseberg.

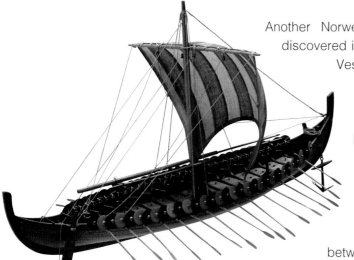

Scale model of the Gokstad ship. Viking Ship Museum, Oslo.

Another Norwegian Viking shipwreck, Gokstad, was discovered in 1880 in a burial mound in the county of Vestfold. This large ship, dated to around 890 by dendrochronology, is also exhibited in the Viking Ship Museum in Oslo. Made of oak, it measured 23.5 metres in length with a 5.2 metre beam and its crew comprised thirty-two oarsmen, whereas its 120 square metre sail enabled it to reach a speed of twelve knots. Contrary to the Oseberg ship, it was designed for the high seas. The skeleton of a man aged between 50 and 70 was found inside the ship, lying on a mortuary bed made of a hollowed-out tree trunk. He may have been one of the Vestfold kings, perhaps Olaf, one of Harald Fairhair's ancestors. His funerary treasure comprised three other smaller boats, a tent, a sleigh and harnessing for a horse. However, it is most likely that this grave was also visited prior to its official discovery for no weapons or metal objects were found.

Other Norwegian ship burials, such as the one discovered in 1852 in Borre (dating from the late 9th – early 10th century) or in 1867 in Tune (dated to around 900), have enabled the history of Viking longships to be retraced up to the early 11th century, when Christianisation resulted in the disappearance of this pagan funerary rite. The Ladby boat, discovered in 1934, is the only funerary wreck to have been found in Denmark, on the island of Funen. A museum is now devoted to the wreck. Dated back to around 925, it measured 21.5 metres in length with a 3 metre beam. No human remains were found, perhaps due to the transfer of any such body to a Christian grave during the 11th century.

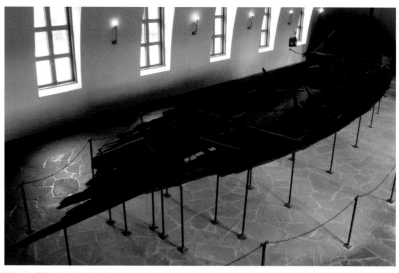

Wreck of the burial ship found in Tune, Norway, displayed in the Viking Ship Museum in Oslo.

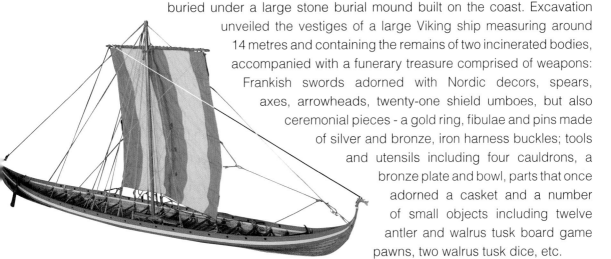

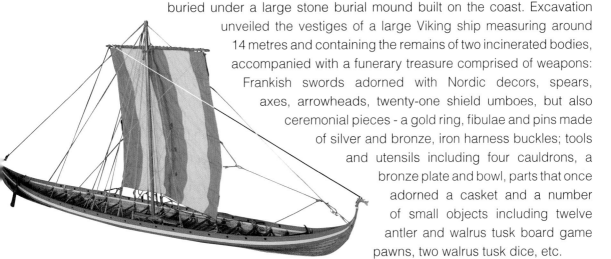

In contrast, the skeletons of eleven horses and four dogs were discovered, as was the ship's iron anchor and chain, along with its prow adorned with sculpted dragons. Archaeologists also unearthed various objects including pieces of dog collar which have enabled dating to be confirmed. The ship's timber features have disappeared and only the mark of the hull, left in the sediment around the burial mound, offers an indication of its measurements, along with the two thousand iron rivets used to attach the clinking.

Archaeological excavation around the Ladby ship in 1935. In the foreground to the right, the remains of horses and the ship's anchor and chain.

Ship burials dating from the Viking Age found outside Scandinavia are quite a rarity. A few were discovered in Scotland, such as the one found in Ardnamurchan, on the west coast of the Scottish mainland, and in Scar, on Sanday, one of the Orkney islands. On the latter side, inside a small 6.6 metre-long *færing* boat, the bodies of an adult couple and a child were found, along with a funerary treasure including a whalebone plaque adorned with two dragon heads, a gilded metal broach and two circular fibulae, a sword and a quiver containing eight arrows, two combs, twenty-two board game pawns, a sickle, a pair of shears and a spindle. The burial took place between 875 and 950. To date, only one ship burial has been discovered in France and not in Normandy as one may suppose, but in Brittany, on the island of Groix near Locmaria, in Morbihan. Discovered in 1906 by Paul du Chatelier and Louis Le Pontois, this Viking sepulchre was buried under a large stone burial mound built on the coast. Excavation unveiled the vestiges of a large Viking ship measuring around 14 metres and containing the remains of two incinerated bodies, accompanied with a funerary treasure comprised of weapons: Frankish swords adorned with Nordic decors, spears, axes, arrowheads, twenty-one shield umboes, but also ceremonial pieces - a gold ring, fibulae and pins made of silver and bronze, iron harness buckles; tools and utensils including four cauldrons, a bronze plate and bowl, parts that once adorned a casket and a number of small objects including twelve antler and walrus tusk board game pawns, two walrus tusk dice, etc.

Scale-model of the Ladby ship, scale 1:10, made by V. Bischoff and K. Jensen. Viking Ship Museum, Oslo.

The collection, dated to the first half of the 10th century, led archaeologists to identify it as the grave of a Viking chief of Norwegian origin, whose possessions illustrate that he had travelled throughout the Western world.

Apart from this grave, there is only one other known Scandinavian sepulchre from the Viking Age in France, this time located in Normandy, upstream of Rouen on the banks of the River Seine: the Pîtres site which, in 1865, unveiled a pair of oval fibulae, in the shape of a "tortoise shell" and dated back to the second half of the 10th century. These two fibulae are exhibited at the Museum of Antiquities in Rouen and are one of the rare vestiges bearing witness to Scandinavian presence in Normandy after Rollo settled there in 911. Yet, they raise more questions than they offer answers. Indeed, we are unaware as to the circumstances of the burial of these fibulae which are exclusively feminine accessories of Norwegian origin. Could they be part of a treasure placed in a larger grave? Today, this sepulchre is believed to have been located on the same site as a 10th century Christian cemetery, for Rollo accepted to convert to Christianity in return for the county of Rouen in 911. So who did these fibulae belong to? Could it be a woman of Scandinavian origin who died after living in Normandy, or a travelling Scandinavian? No one knows...

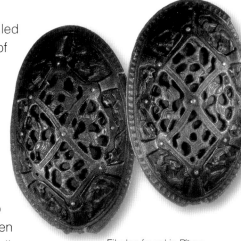

Fibulae found in Pîtres.

Whale bone plaque discovered in the Scar ship burial site in Sanday, Orkney.

Ardnamurchan ship burial mound, west coast of the Highlands, Scotland.

The Skuldelev ships

Over and above the aforementioned ship burials, Scandinavian archaeologists also made an extraordinary discovery: that of the five Skuldelev ships, found in the Danish fjord of Roskilde and today exhibited to curious visitors from across the globe at the Viking Ship Museum where they are preserved along with their identical replicas. In the early 11th century, Roskilde was the capital of the Kings of Denmark. The town nestles at the far end of a deep fjord, the sea access to which was blocked by a barrier of stakes, positioned at Skuldelev, at a narrowing in the channel around ten nautical miles to the north of Roskilde. Around 1030, threatening ships managed to enter the fjord and sailed up towards the town. Lookouts immediately informed the Skuldelev villagers who scuttled several ships filled with stones in order to block the channel entrance, hence preventing the enemy from approaching. A thousand years later, in 1957, a team of archaeologists undertook to bring back to the surface these wrecks of which local tradition had maintained vague memories. They identified the vestiges of five ships from the Viking Age, two of which were armed for warfare, two equipped for trade and the last one for fishing or coastal navigation. This exceptional discovery bears witness to the Scandinavians' great talent in naval construction in the early 11th century, i.e. thirty years before the Norman Conquest of England. Their ships were high-performance models, designed for a number of different uses and of remarkable efficiency and unrivalled economy of means.

Archaeological excavation of *Skuldelev 5*, 1962.

Archaeological excavation in Skuldelev, 1962.

Scale model of *Skuldelev 5*, a *snekkja* boat, made by V. Bischoff and E. Andersen. Viking Ship Museum, Roskilde.

The Skulðelev ships

Skuldelev 1 was a high-seas *knarr*, of a length of 15.8 metres and a beam of 4.8 metres, decked at its extremities and with an open hold in the middle. Originally built of pine around 1030 in the west of Norway, it was repaired several times using oak in the Oslo fjord and in eastern Denmark. It could transport six to eight men, carry a load of 20 tonnes and its 90 square metre sail offered it a speed of up to 13 knots. The *Ottar* is its replica.

Skuldelev 2 was a large Viking warship, referred to as a *skeið*, of a length of 30 metres and a beam of 3.8 metres, capable of transporting 65 to 70 men and a load of 26 tonnes. It was made of oak in the Dublin region around 1042. Its slender hull, sixty oarholes and 112 square metre sail rendered it a versatile and fast ship, capable of reaching a speed of 17 knots. The *Sea Stallion of Glendalough* is its replica.

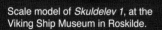

Scale model of *Skuldelev 1*, at the Viking Ship Museum in Roskilde.

Skuldelev 3 was a small versatile *byrding* boat of a length of 14 metres and a beam of 3.3 metres, built around 1040 using Danish oak. Its two extremities were equipped with a mobile deck, whereas its middle section had an open hold. It could transport five to eight men with a total load capacity of 9.6 tonnes. It was well-adapted to suit the seafaring conditions in the Danish waters and the Baltic Sea, driven essentially by sail (45 square metres) and reaching a maximum speed of 8 to 10 knots. The *Roar Ege* is its replica.

The variety of vessels discovered in Skuldelev by archaeologists illustrates that the notion of a Viking boat necessarily comprises a great diversity of vessels that can be distinguished from each other by their varying dimensions and construction materials, based on their construction site, the seas they were to sail and the tasks for which they were designed. For indeed, the Vikings sailed on several types of ship that were divided by the great naval archaeologist Ole Crumlin-Pedersen into two major families: firstly, the *langskip,* designed for war and Viking raids and, secondly, the *kaupskip*, a sturdier vessel designed for transport

Iron rivets found in the Oseberg ship.

Skuldelev 5 was a small *snekkja* warfaring boat, of a length of 17.3 metres and a beam of 2.5 metres and equipped with thirteen benches. It was built around 1030 using oak, ash and pine recovered from other vessels. It could transport thirty men for a total load capacity of 7.8 tonnes. The hull's upper planking was equipped with holes for leather shield straps. Its 46 square metre sail offered the boat a speed of up to 15 knots. The *Helge Ask* is its replica.

The Sea Stallion, a replica of *Skuldelev 2*, navigating under sail in 2008.

Skuldelev 6 was a fishing boat made of Norwegian pine, birch and oak around 1030 and of a length of 11.2 metres for a beam of 2.5 metres. Its planking was later raised in order to increase its load capacity, hence the disappearance of the oar supports. Its crew, initially comprised of fifteen men for seven pairs of oars, was consequently reduced to five men. Its 26.5 square metre sail enabled this ship to transport its three tonne cargo at a speed of nine to twelve knots. The *Kraka Fyr* is its replica.

Kraka fyr, a replica of Skuldelev 6, Roskilde Fjord, Denmark.

Anchors represented on the Bayeux Tapestry. Scenes 5 and 34.

and trade. *Langskips* were decked and transported more rowers than *kaupskips*, whose hull was specifically designed to carry the ship's cargo. They both navigated by sail or by oar and their slender hulls, of a low draught, enabled them to sail up rivers or to easily ground on beaches and river banks. They were given different names depending on their size. The largest were referred to as *karv* (singular *karfi*), the Oseberg ship being a fine example. They were used in particular as ceremonial ships. In the same family, *snekkja* were smaller, but also much faster and easier to manoeuvre. Their name later gave way to the Normandy "esneque". *Kaupskips* were not entirely decked and generally navigated by sail with a smaller crew. Depending on their size and their load capacity, they were referred to as *byrdings* or *knarrs*. During the Viking Age, there were also other small working boats equipped for fishing and coastal navigation, such as the *færing,* the *skúta* and the *ferja* whose name later gave way to the English word ferry.

Despite their many differences, all these ships were built according to the same architectural design. Their lightweight, long and narrow hull, the extremities of which were symmetrically raised, was clinker-built, generally using oak, and attached to the boat's frame by means of metallic circular

Rudders represented on the Bayeux Tapestry. Scenes 5 and 38.

or oval sectioned rivets. Watertightness was ensured by means of wool, horse hair and tar caulking. Their only sail was rectangular, hoisted onto a pine mast and held in place by a mobile wooden beam which offered great flexibility against the violent gusts of the north winds. The rigging was made of ropes and seal skins. The boat was steered by means of a large side rudder equipped with a steering oar. It had a wrought iron anchor and the top of the mast was sometimes adorned with a metal weather vane. A large Viking ship could transport sixty armed men. Its captain and owner was also the steersman, considered as a prestigious position, even up to William the Conqueror's time. Life on board this type of ship was harsh; there was no cabin, just a tautened canvas behind the mast, and the men, who were seated on their chest by day, slept two by two in a watertight leather bag. The hull enabled water, food, goods and even horses to be loaded. Horses were trained to embark and disembark, as represented on "life size" replicas of Viking boats, reproduced by Scandinavian archaeologists. There is there-fore no reason to doubt the Normans' capacity to do likewise in 1066... Indeed, the Bayeux Tapestry clearly illustrates how this could be done and we also know to what extent the Norman horsemen were equestrian experts.

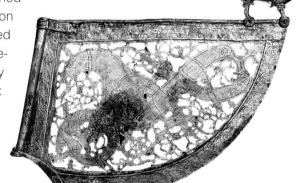

Heggen weathervane, in gilded copper, 11th century.

These small Icelandic horses were taken to the island aboard Norwegian ships in the 9th century...

Landing horses as depicted on the Bayeux Tapestry. Scene 30.

The Norwegians in the Northwest

The first official Viking raids in history were led by Norwegians in particular. They came from Norway via the Orkney and Shetlands islands, where they very quickly established permanent settlements, to begin their pillaging on the northeast coast of England in 793, before heading northwards round Scotland, reaching the Irish Sea as early as 795. The same year, they attacked Iona Abbey, in the Inner Hebrides, along with the monastery on Lambey Island to the north of Dublin. Over their repeated incursions, year by year, every spring, the Vikings infested all the Scottish and Irish estuaries, attacking small and poorly defended harbour towns. At the time, Ireland was divided into small kingdoms that were incapable of implementing efficient defensive systems against these opportunist pillagers from the North. Over the years, the Norwegians established a regular route for their pillaging, bypassing Scotland to the north, where they established seasonal or temporary bases in the Shetlands, Orkney and the Hebrides.

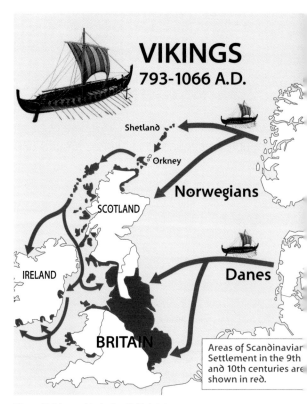

Map of Viking raids in the British Isles.

Scotland

In Scotland, the Vikings began by attacking the monks on the Isle of Skye and on Iona, before establishing bases that offered them seasonal shelter along the coast. The Norwegian jarls very quickly founded small seigniories in Orkney and the Hebrides, as well as the Isle of Man, where they lived in Scandinavian style. Some of the rare ship burials outside Scandinavia have been discovered there. This area was of crucial importance to the Norwegian Vikings for whom Scotland and its islands were a necessary stopover on their expedition route. We know that Harald Fairhair waged war there, as did his great grandson, Olaf Tryggvason, also King of Norway from 995 to 1000. Another figure, the son of an Orkney jarl, also made a name for himself in Scotland: Hrólf (aka Rollo), apparently no less than the future founder of the very first Normandy... All these chiefs, whatever their importance, engaged in pillaging. The Christian sanctuary of Iona, pillaged for the first time in 795, was attacked repeatedly. The local population, a medley of Britons, Scots and Picts, were incapable of challenging such a threat. In northern Scotland, the

Pictish kings were quickly overthrown by the Vikings and, around 843, the King of Scots Kenneth MacAlpin reunited both crowns, founding the great Kingdom of Alba. In Strathclyde, in the west of Scotland, Britons were caught in a pincer movement between the Vikings established in the Hebrides and those in Ireland, led by Olaf the White from the longphort of Dublin.

In 870, Olaf's troops, who allied with those of the King of Alba, besieged the fortress of Dumbarton, - the capital of the kings of Strathclyde - for four months before successfully seizing the stronghold. Henceforth, the Hebridean Vikings integrated the Kingdom of the Britons. In 871, Olaf returned triumphantly to Dublin with a fleet of two hundred ships laden with slaves and spoils and made a pact with the kings of the Scots and of Strathclyde. A Viking county was founded in Orkney around 880. Then followed a relatively calm period in Scotland, during which the Kingdom of Alba gradually and intelligently developed with its new Norwegian neighbours. After successive ransacking, Iona Abbey continued its activity. Around the year 1000, its monks produced what may be one of the most admirable masterpieces of Western medieval intellectual and artistic history: the Book of Kells, an illuminated evangelistary which owes its name to an Irish abbey located in the county of Meath. The same period saw the emergence of a hybrid culture born from the integration of Scandinavians in this part of Scotland. This is why a King of Alba came to bear a name of Norse origin...

Archaeological excavation in a Viking house in Skaill, Sandwick in Orkney.

Aerial view of the Brough of Deerness site, Orkney.

Ireland

Throughout the 9th century, the Norwegian expeditions in the Irish Sea became increasingly important. On the Emerald Isle, they undertook to establish permanent residences, in the form of fortified ports referred to as "longphorts", from which they led their expeditions inland and on both shores of the Irish Sea. The two oldest longphorts appear to have been founded in 841 in Dublin and in Linn Dúachaill, today called Annagassan, in the county of Lough, at the mouth of the Glyde. These two sites were followed by others, at the origin of the first Irish towns: Dublin, but also Waterford, Wexford, Cork and Limerick, located in the south. In Dublin, archaeologists have unearthed graves, vestiges of houses made of pleated wood and Scandinavian objects. Recently, they even discovered the ditches that protected the Viking longphort, which served equally as a place of residence, a port and a marketplace with other, more distant Viking lands.

The Vikings sailed up rivers, infiltrating inland Ireland and threatening its Gaelic kingdoms. This crisis forced the Irish people and their sovereigns to reunite their efforts. In 845, Máel Sechnaill mac Domnaill, King of Mide, had his men capture a notorious Viking chief by the name of Thorgils, who was chief of the longphort of Dublin. From his stronghold, Thorgils had taken the habit of launching raids throughout Ireland and Wales, making use, along his way, of a series of small forts established inland, in the banks of the lakes Lough Ree and Lough Lene. To make an example of him, the King of Mide sentenced Thorgils to death by drowning in the deep waters of Lough Owel, a vast lake to the west of the town. This was to earn the Gaelic king great prestige, which he exploited by compelling recognition from his like.

Lough Owel to the west of Dublin. Some of the lake's small islands were visibly used as small forts by the Dublin Vikings.

However, in the meantime, the Danes had despatched an army to Ireland in order to unseat the Norwegian Vikings. In 852, they won a major battle against them at Carlingford, in the county of Lough, to the north of Dublin. This is when a new Viking chief from Norway entered the scene – Olaf the White (*Hvitr*). In 853, he led a powerful fleet to regain control of the longphort of Dublin, immediately resuming operations in the Irish Sea along with his brother Ivarr. Olaf was looking to seize power throughout Ireland. Colluding with their fathers, he married at least three Gaelic princesses before capturing the towns of Armagh in 869. Hence, Olaf reigned over a vast share of Ireland, and probably also the Hebrides and Wales, until his last return trip to Norway in 871. He left his territories to his brother Ivarr, who survived him by two years. Under their reign, the Norwegians settled on the island; however, the Viking kingdom of Dublin did not survive them for long, for the Irish regained the advantage as they gradually joined forces. The town was reconquered in 902 and the Vikings were driven out.

Set of swords found in the 19th century in the Kilmainham Viking cemetery, a former settlement located to the west of Dublin. National Museum of Ireland.

Dumbarton Castle - Scotland, built on the rock that overlooks the present-day town since at least the Iron Age. The Dublin Vikings siezed the site in 870 after a four month siege.

Sculpture of Brian Boru, Chapel Royal, Dublin Castle.

For another century, the Viking chiefs descended from Ivarr continued their efforts to conquer Ireland and to reunite it with their other settlements in Scotland and, to a greater extent, in England. It was a century of incessant warfare during which power passed from hand to hand, until the decisive Battle of Clontarf in 1014, won by Brian Boru and his Irish troops. Brian Boru (circa 941-1014) was the son and heir of the King of Thomond, an area located in the north of the province of Munster. Throughout his youth, he battled with the Vikings, successfully recovering Limerick in 976, before gradually asserting his authority throughout Munster, Leinster and the Kingdom of Dublin. His success aroused dreams of wearing a unified Irish crown. In the spring of 1014, his Gaelic rivals formed a coalition against him. They included his own brother Mael Mordha, King of Leinster, and the Irish-Norwegian King of Dublin, Sigtrygg Silkbeard (*Silkislegg*), the son of Olaf the White with one of his Gaelic wives. They had benefited from support from the Viking lords in Orkney and the Hebrides whom Sigtrygg had called upon for help. On Good Friday, on the 23rd of April 1014, Brian Boru had himself crowned "High King of Ireland" by his troops, before meeting with the Clontarf coalition near Dublin, where his army of twenty thousand men won an overwhelming victory, leaving seven thousand Norwegians dead on the battlefield. However, Brian, aged 73, also lost his life, murdered in his tent by a Viking.

After the Clontarf disaster, the Norwegians abandoned their political ambitions in Ireland and limited their efforts to commercial activities from the longphorts of Dublin, Wexford, Cork and Limerick, which they continued to control for many years to come. Their small communities were gradually integrated within Ireland, which nevertheless remained divided into a large number of principalities. They brought with them many Scandinavian influences: their skill for naval construction and navigation, Nordic poetry and many words of Old Norse origin which can still be found in place and personal names.

The Battle of Clontarf, by Hugh Frazer, 1826.

Northwar∂s!

After leading raids in the north of the British Isles and the Irish Sea, the Norwegians ventured further northwest, sailing towards the Faroe Islands, then to Iceland and beyond, towards Greenland and America.

The Faroe Islands

Located to the far north of Scotland, the Faroe Islands were almost virgin territory, inhabited only by a handful of Irish monks. The Vikings baptised them the "islands of sheep" (*Frœreyjar*), which offers a clear indication of their key use: to offer a stopping place on the grand maritime expedition route towards the great north, sheep being the main source of winter nourishment. The *Faereyinga Saga* (Norse saga of the Faroemen), written in the early 13th century, is the leading reference work offering a comprehensive history of the Vikings in the Faroe Islands. Toponymy and archaeology have provided precious information that can be crossed with this work, written several centuries after the events themselves.

Runestone exhibited in Sandavágur church on Vagar Island, in the Faroe Islands. The stone's inscription, dating from the 13th century, perpetuates the memory of a Viking chief of Norwegian origin by the name of Thorkell: 'Thorkell son of Onundr, a man from the east of Rogaland, was the first to live here'.

Typical landscape in the Faroe Islands: the small town of Klaksvik, on the island of Borðoy, is the second most important after the capital, Tórshavln. Colourful houses nestle round the harbour in the depths of a fjord surrounded by high and freezing mountains. Nearby, a few hardy sheep graze. They were brought to the islands by the Nordic colonists.

According to the *Faereyinga Saga*, Grimm Kamban was the first Viking to settle in the archipelago in 825. Grimm may have been among the Vikings that had fled Norway to escape King Harald Fairhair's condemnation. Indeed, when he took the throne of Norway, Harald immediately set to pacifying his kingdom, banishing many Vikings, who were forced to flee Scandinavia and to head for the Scottish isles, Ireland and the Faroe Islands. However, Grimm's family name, Kamban, is of Celtic consonance which suggests he may have been

Archaeological excavation of a Viking house in Á Sondum on the island of Sandoy in the Faroe Islands by archaeologists from Durham University in England.

of Irish-Norwegian origin. Whatever, he settled in Funningur to the northwest of the island of Eysturoy, where archaeologists did indeed discover a group of houses of the Nordic style. Grimm could not have lived alone on his island. In the first half of the 9th century, several families from Norway or from the Norwegian settlements in northern Scotland and the Irish Sea settled in the Faroe Islands, building farms, growing wheat and breeding sheep - which grazed on the short grass - and a few cattle. Since no tree grows in these high latitudes, they heated their homes with peat which formed in the marshes by plant decomposition. Extracted in blocks then dried, it offered an efficient alternative to wood. Construction timber was nevertheless an architectural feature of the Viking houses in the Faroe Islands. For example, on the island of Streymoy, archaeological excavation has unearthed the vestiges of a twenty metre-long Viking farm covered with a vast timber roof. Analyses have proven that the wood used to build it was imported by boat from Norway.

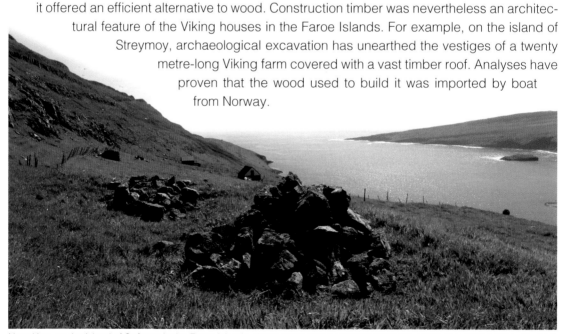

Near Hov, on the island of Suðuroy in the Faroe Islands, these stone burial mounds mark the grave of a Viking chief, of whom tradition has preserved the name: Havgrimur.

Iceland

Around 850, the Vikings established in the Faroe islands learned of the existence of a large deserted island located in the far north: Iceland. The story of the Norwegians' settlement in Iceland is told in a major literary work, the *Book of Icelanders* (*Íslendingabók*), written in the 12th century by an Icelandic monk of the name of Ari Thorgilsson. A little later, in the late 13th century, another book, the *Book of Settlements* (*Landnámabók*) details the history of the first Icelandic colonists. As in the Faroe Islands, archaeology now enables us to match and verify the information provided by these books which were written a long time after the events they cover.

The Norwegians discovered Iceland by chance and probably thanks to information provided by the Irish, for small groups of monks had already sailed to the island for short stays a century earlier. Around 850, a Viking called Naddothur lost his way amidst the seas on his way to the Faroe Islands, perhaps due to a storm. He finally landed on the east coast of Iceland, an icy cold country which he baptised "Land of snow". A little later, another Viking of Swedish origin, Gardar Svavarsson, followed the same route and travelled round the island which he took possession of and rebaptised "Island of Gardar". He then spent the winter on the north coast where he founded the Húsavík "House bay" settlement, leaving the island and abandoning three of his slaves there. A little later, the *Landnámabók* told of a Viking named Flóki Vilgerdarson, who sailed one day from the Faroe Islands to reach an island that a handful of sailors before him had spotted to the northwest. As he left the Faroe Islands, he set free three crows which were supposed to guide him to dry land.

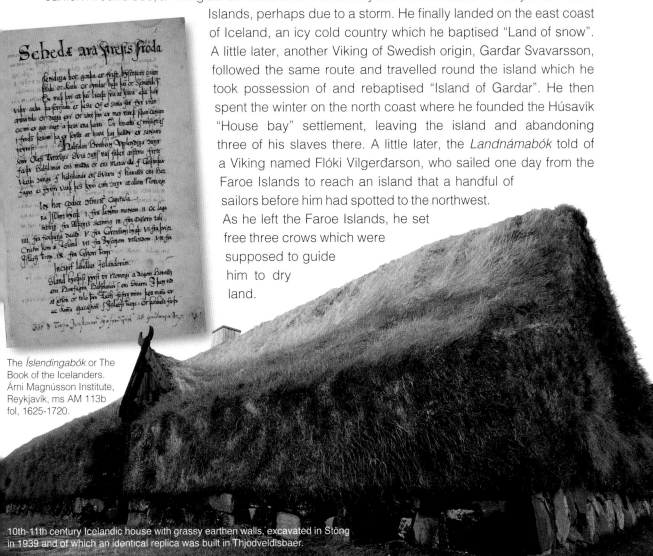

The *Íslendingabók* or The Book of the Icelanders. Árni Magnússon Institute, Reykjavík, ms AM 113b fol, 1625-1720.

10th-11th century Icelandic house with grassy earthen walls, excavated in Stöng in 1939 and of which an identical replica was built in Thjodveldisbaer.

Two returned to the boat, but not the third. Hence, Flóki, henceforth nicknamed "Flóki of the Crows" (Hrafna-Flóki), continued his journey until he reached an unknown island. He set foot on dry land within a large bay where he settled for a very harsh winter with his companions. The following spring, he explored the surrounding area and climbed a mountain. From the summit, he observed a frozen fjord and named the country: Iceland... After a second equally cold winter, he returned to the Faroe Islands.

This episode preceded the island's true colonisation, which began during the 870s. Despite its extremely cold winters, Iceland was at the time a fertile land, covered with birch trees, with a wealth of iron and hot springs, of fish, seals and whales. In a few decades, several hundred families – Scandinavian and Faroese peasants – settled along the coast and the plains in the south of the island. The volcanic mountains that form the island's centre remained uninhabited. As in the Shetlands and the Faroe Islands, archaeological excavation has offered proof of colonies living in large house-stables with very thick walls, made of stone and earth and covered with peat and grass mounds, which offered maximum insulation during the winter. Yet, in very little time, ground clearing and sheep grazing destroyed the birch forest which never grew again.

Iceland's colonisation continued till the 930s, reaching its peak at around six thousand inhabitants, whose names, which are listed in 12th and 13th century books, indicated that they originated from southwest Norway and from the Norwegian settlements in the British Isles. This small Icelandic society very quickly adopted the Scandinavian way of life. Large families then founded a community that was independent from the Kingdom of Norway, with its own parliament, the Althing, comprised of the most popular family chiefs, and its own capital, Reykjavík, whose name in Old Norse means "Bay of Smokes", after the steam that emanates from the region's many hot springs. During the 10th century, the Icelanders lived a peaceful and relatively prosperous life thanks to the product of agriculture, fishing and Viking expeditions. They developed an original culture which is retraced in the sagas written by Snorri Sturluson, which were the heirs to the oral tradition of the first colonists.

'Ingolf tager Island i besiddelse' - the foundation of Reykjavík by Ingólfr Arnarson in 824. Painting by P. Raadsig, 1850.

The Saga of Erik the Red tells of the discovery of Greenland and of its first colonists. MF 544, 4, *Hauksbó*, early 14th century.

Greenland

The Norwegians' northbound adventures were far from over. In 982, the Viking Erik Thorvaldsson, known as Erik the Red (circa 940 or 950-1003 or 1010) was banished from Iceland for murder. We know of his expedition thanks to the *Saga of Erik the Red,* written by a 13th century Icelandic cleric whose works include several previously drafted Icelandic tales.

Erik was the son of a Norwegian Viking of the name of Thorvald Asvalsson, himself banished from Norway for murder. Around 970, Thorvald settled with his family in northwest Iceland. This is where his son, Erik, heard of the travels of another Norwegian, Gunnbjörn Ulfsson, who discovered the rocky isles to the west, in Greenland's region of Ammasalik… In 978, it was Snæbjörn Galti's turn to head for Greenland with a handful of colonists. Snæbjörn had planned to settle their; however, his expedition met with a catastrophic end. During a violent quarrel, he was assassinated by one of his crew members.

Some time later, Erik the Red was in turn banished for murder and decided to try his luck in this unknown land to the west. He left Iceland and sailed due west for a long time before spotting a coast amidst the icebergs. Further afield, he sailed past a headland to discover verdant fjords which whispered to him the name of Greenland. This detail is indicative of the period's climate warming, referred to by specialists as the "small climate optimum". This large-scale movement particularly affected the maritime routes used by the Vikings, both in northern Europe and towards the

Specialists have retraced the history of Greenland's former climate by studying its peat bogs.

The Lewis chessmen, carved in walrus ivory (12th century).

great north, for it led to a retreat of the ice floe and periods of thawing propitious to the development of vegetation. This mild period continued to the 12th century to be followed by a period of cooling throughout, referred to as the little ice age and the effects of which impacted the climate up to the 19th century.

Erik the Red stayed in Greenland for three years, exploring part of the coast. He then decided to return to Iceland to gather a fleet of twenty-five ships, transporting five hundred colonists. The convoy set sail the following spring; however, only fifteen boats reached their destination unscathed. Others arrived later, to reach a total of five thousand settlers. They were welcomed to two settlements, located in the depths of the fjords on the west coast, one in Eystribygg and the other in Vestribygg, the site of the present-day towns of Nuuk and Qaqortoq. These early Greenlanders lived in extreme conditions, adopting the Icelandic lifestyle. Erik became their chief and, following the example of his wife Thiordhild, a certain number of them converted to Christianity and built a church. The colony lived on fishing and on fur, walrus tusk and narwhal tusk trade with Iceland. However, around 1010, a serious epidemic decimated the population, among whom Erik the Red. Greenland's Viking settlements survived until the late 14th century, despite dramatic climate changes and difficult relationships with the Eskimos which they called "*Skrælings*".

Disko Bay in Greenland, where archaeologists have unearthed walrus tusks dating from the Viking Age.

61

The Vikings in America!

Around the year 1000, one of Erik the Red's son's Leif Erikson (circa 970-circa 1025), undertook a new exploratory journey ever further west. As had probably been the case of his father, he was told of the tales of Bjarni Herjólfsson, an Icelandic explorer, who claimed to have spotted land in that direction around 986. Leif sailed due west, first to reach an icy coast which he baptised Helluland: the "land of flat stones", today home to Baffin Island and the north of Labrador. He then discovered another land, this time verdant and wooded, which he called Markland or "land of the trees". This time, he had undoubtedly reached the south of Labrador. He continued to finally reach a third verdant coast where he decided to set up camp for the winter: he called it Vinland, the "land of vines", after the wild berries that Leif's companions discovered on site.

The Greenlanders initially named their settlement "Leifsbuthir", meaning "Leif's houses". It has been suggested that the site was located in Waquoit Bay on the south coast of Cape Cod, in the state of Massachusetts, in the vicinity of the famous resort of Nantucket. It could also have been in Bay St. Lawrence, to the north of Cape Breton Island in Nova Scotia; however, no archaeological excavation has been undertaken, in contrast with the third theory: L'Anse aux Meadows on the island of Newfoundland. On the latter site, in the 1950s, archaeologists discovered the unquestionable vestiges of a Viking camp. Nevertheless, certain historians believe this to be a base established by one of Leif Erikson's followers, rather than Leif himself. Similarly, excavation work has also been undertaken on Baffin Island, in northern Canada, unveiling the marks of beams and stonework, objects made of iron, bone and sculpted wood, sharpening stones, woven wool and ropes, not forgetting... European rat hair, proving the presence of a European settlement, five centuries before Christopher Columbus!

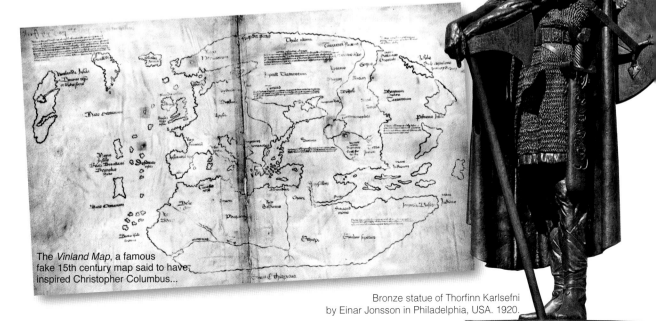

The *Vinland Map*, a famous fake 15th century map said to have inspired Christopher Columbus...

Bronze statue of Thorfinn Karlsefni by Einar Jonsson in Philadelphia, USA. 1920.

Upon his return to Greenland, Leif very quickly succeeded his father at the head of the community. Some of his close relations then launched a new expedition to Vinland. The *Saga of the Greenlanders*, written before 1300 and based on old oral tradition, later tells of another Viking, Thorfinn Karlsefni, who sailed to Vinland with two of Leif's brothers. He settled there with 160 colonists including sixteen women, in search of fur and, more importantly, wood which was in great demand in Iceland. However, they were to face great hostility from the American Indians who forced them to retreat to the Straumfjörd site. The sagas portray a land with a climate slightly milder than today's, which is perfectly in line with what we know of the Little Climate Optimum (aka Medieval Warm Period). The Vinland colonists grew vine and wild wheat, chopped wood and fished abundant quantities of salmon. However, many were soon to fall under Skræling arrows, and Thorfinn decided to return to Greenland. The Viking settlements in Canada and North America were abandoned for evermore...

L'Anse aux Meaðows

L'Anse aux Meadows is an archaeological site located to the north of the Canadian island of Newfoundland, in the province of Newfoundland and Labrador. From 1961 to 1968, a couple of Norwegian archaeologists, Anne Stine and Helge Instad, along with an international team of Americans and Scandinavians, unearthed the vestiges of a Viking settlement which succeeded several other, older encampments occupied by American Indians. The vestiges comprise eight buildings including a forge and a wood chopping workshop, associated with a naval construction yard, together with several objects, fifty of which are made of metal and all of typical Scandinavian style. The site appears to have been occupied briefly, over a few years. This discovery had the effect of a bombshell and several voices were raised to challenge this interpretation which called into question the primacy of Christopher Columbus' discovery. Yet, over later years, other Viking settlements were discovered on Baffin Island and in Labrador, hence clearly confirming the presence of small Scandinavian groups on North-American territory around the year 1000. Excavation work in L'Anse aux Meadows was resumed under the aegis of the Canadian government from 1973 to 1976 and the site was eventually listed as a UNESCO World Heritage site, as the supposed location of the almost legendary colony founded by Leif Erikson in Vinland. Nevertheless, certain historians believe it was a different settlement, called Straumfjörd and founded by Thorfinn Karlsefni. This is where his son, Snorri, upon his birth, became the very first European to be born in the New World.

Reproduction of the Viking house in Jarlshof, Shetland, on the L'anse aux Meadows site.

The Danes in England and the Channel

In the wake of the Vikings from Norway, those from Denmark approached the east coast of England where their early raids very quickly became large-scale operations that supplanted those led by the Norwegians. From the Thames and other eastern estuaries, they headed inland towards the Anglo-Saxon kingdoms of East Anglia, Mercia and Northumbria

The Danelaw

In 850, the Danes captured the towns of London and Canterbury then, in 865, the author of the *Anglo-Saxon Chronicle* reported that a large Viking army had come from Denmark to conquer the north of England. Two years later, the Danes took the town of York, the capital of Northumbria.

Map of the battles waged by the Great Danish Army in England.

They founded the capital of a new territory there: the Danelaw, initially limited to the north of England then extended southwards. York, rebaptised Jorvík, was home to a large craft and trade hub with connections with the English Channel and the North Sea. The Vikings took advantage of this major asset, bringing in hundreds of immigrants from Denmark. In the town centre, archaeologists have discovered a range of objects imported by the Danes, bearing witness to their immigration and the long-distant trade links established by the Danelaw Vikings across the globe.

Of all the Anglo-Saxon sovereigns, only the powerful King of Wessex, Alfred the Great (871-899) was still capable of stopping them in their tracks. In May 878, he crushed the Danelaw troops at the Battle of Eddington. Then followed the signing of a treaty in Wedmore, and the King of Danelaw's acceptance to be christened as Alfred's godson. Nevertheless, their accord was short-lived and hostilities rapidly resumed, in favour of the Anglo-Saxons, who managed to reconquer London in 885. After his death, Alfred the Great's son and successor,

Statue of Alfred the Great in Winchester by Hamo Thornycroft, 1899.

Edward the Elder, depicted on the illuminated manuscript Royal 14 BVI, containing the family tree of the Kings of England. British Library, London, early 14th century.

Edward the Elder (899-924), pursued his efforts by regaining control of the former kingdoms of East Anglia and Mercia, at a cost of a bitter battle against, not only the Danes, but also his Anglo-Saxon rivals who readily rallied with the Vikings. In 910, he won the Battle of Tetenhall, with help from Æthelred, Lord of the Mercians. Vikings landed in the Severn in south Wales before heading inland into Mercia which they ransacked. They were led by the kings of Danelaw, Halfdan and Eowils, who had allied with Ivarr, the Viking chief of Dublin Olaf the White's brother. Laden with spoils, they headed northwards to the Danelaw, believing Edward to be in Kent, busy reuniting a fleet. However, in the meantime, the King of Wessex had obtained support from Mercia and the two armies succeeded in surrounding the Danes, inflicting a bitter defeat upon them and killing both the Danelaw kings. Hence, Edward finally drove the Danes above the natural frontier marked by the Humber, a vast estuary on the east coast of England. Then, in 911, he annexed the cities of London and Oxford, in order to gain control of the entire centre of England. To consolidate his positions in the north, Edward ordered for the construction of several fortified towns, referred to as "*burhs*", in Herford, Witham and Bridgnorth, along with a series of forts to prevent the Danes from reconquering former territories. Nine years later, Northumbria was finally totally under control and, by the end of his reign, Edward was acknowledged as overlord of Scotland.

Rampart and enclosure ditch of the Wallingford *burh*, in Oxfordshire, founded under Edward the Elder.

The Danelaw, know reduced to its early territory, was henceforth controlled by the Vikings of Ireland. In 948, the Danes of Jorvik called upon the bloodthirsty King of Norway, Eric Bloodaxe, who, since chased from the throne by his brother Håkon, readily became their leader in England. At constant rivalry with Eadred of Wessex and Olaf of Dublin, Eric upheld his position up to his violent death during the Battle of Stainmore in 954 against troops led by Olaf's son, Magnus. These fratricide battles between Viking chiefs clearly demonstrate to what extent there was no national or ethnic unity between the native populations and Scandinavian groups who, to gain power, battled equally against each other as against foreign adversaries. After 954, the Anglo-Saxons drove the Vikings out of the Danelaw and England enjoyed a relatively peaceful period up to the late 10th century.

From the Frankish coasts to the Mediterranean

The Danes entered the English Channel before the official date of 793 since their presence is mentioned to the south of the Isle of Portland as early as 789. In 808 and 810, King Godfred defied Charlemagne by sending two large expeditions against his Slavic and Frisian vassals in the Baltic Sea and the North Sea. Since the Franks had no fleet, their Frisian vassals were technically in charge of sea traffic between the North Sea and the Channel. Dorestad, their major port, was located on the mouth of the Rhine, today in the Netherlands. The immense site covered a surface area of thirty hectares round the river. In 810, the Danish fleet, which comprised

Sumptuous fibula of Burgundian origin discovered in Dorestad in 1969, dated circa 800.

two hundred drakkars, ravaged the port which was subsequently pillaged every year from 834 to 837, then from 846 to 847 and from 857 to 863. Meanwhile, from 841 to 873, the Holy Roman Emperor Lothair entrusted his Friesland government to a Danish lord of the name of Rorik in exchange for his loyalty and, in particular, for the region's defence against other Vikings.

The port of Quentovic, at the Channel entrance, met with a similar fate. Located on the mouth of the River Canche, near the small village of La Calotterie, in Pas-de-Calais, the site enjoyed intense and regular traffic with the British, Frisian and Scandinavian worlds. Around 800, along with Dorestad and Southampton, it was one of the three largest commercial ports in Northwest Europe, under Charlemagne and his heirs' direct control. Yet, in 840 and 842, the Danes ravaged Quentovic twice over, to return there in 864, 881, 890 and 894. The port ceased all activity in the year 1000.

Carolingian treasure discovered in Dorestad. Dorestad Museum.

Jumièges Abbey, pieces of charred wood and capitals bearing the marks of a fire.

The Danes then concentrated their efforts along the Frankish and Gallic coast. After an early incursion within the Seine estuary in 820, they returned there every spring as from 840. In May 841, their drakkars ravaged Rouen and Jumièges, whilst another contingent ransacked the city of Chartres. Rich monasteries were a choice target for the Vikings. To save their skins, the monks of Saint-Wandrille handed over great quantities of gold, whereas those from Saint-Denis, to the north of Paris, paid a heavy ransom in exchange for the release of sixty prisoners. A fortnight later, laden with spoils, the Northmen headed back to sea; however, their success spurred them to return the following year. In 843, they entered the Loire area. In Nantes, they murdered Bishop Gohard, before settling on the island of Noirmoutier, where their chief colluded with the Count of Nantes, who had been deprived of his title by Charles the Bald (823-877), and with the Breton King Nominoe, already in control of Cotentin and keen to conquer what was later to become Normandy. However, their army was crushed by the Franks at Messac, in Ille-et-Vilaine. This did not prevent the Vikings from sailing up the Garonne the following year, from pillaging Agen and threatening Toulouse, whilst trying to conquer Seville, only to be driven back by the Emir of Cordoba!

In 845, a Viking army launched the first major raid on Paris, whilst others attacked Charente. The following year, the Noirmoutier Vikings headed inland of the Loire Valley. From 848 to 850, the Danes captured Bordeaux, Périgueux and Auch then, as from 851, these "kings of the sea" spent several winters in the low valleys of the Loire and the Seine, as in the small Norman estuaries such as the Dives... Permanent bases were established near Rouen, on the islands of Jeufosse and Oissel, which in 1030 was still referred to as *Thorhulmus*, "Thor's island" in a charter by Robert the Magnificent. Whilst the terrorised monastic communities began a massive inland exodus, taking with them their precious relics, the Viking violence reached its peak in 855. After ransacking Bordeaux once more, the Danes besieged Paris for the second time in 856, whilst the Charente Vikings headed on horseback towards Clermont-Ferrand, in the centre of the Massif Central! From 858 to 860, two Danish fleets sailed along the Atlantic coast to attack the Iberian Peninsula, in A Coruña, Porto, Lisbon, Seville, Cordoba and Cádiz, before crossing the Straits of Gibraltar and entering the Mediterranean, where they ransacked several North African villages. They then spent the winter in the Rhone delta, which one fleet sailed up whilst another attacked Italy, to continue its travels as far as Constantinople!

The Frankish kings were powerless against such a threat. Lacking a permanent fleet, the coast was poorly defended and the troubles kindled separatist ambitions, particularly in Aquitaine. To protect his kingdom to the west, Charles the Bald, who succeeded Louis the Pious in 843, conceded the county of Cotentin to the Breton King Salomon, in exchange for his support against the Vikings. He also ordered the construction of fortified bridges over the rivers, in particular at the confluence of the Eure and the Seine, near his palace in Pîtres, in order to prevent the Vikings from sailing towards Paris. The huge construction campaign lasted a decade, from 862 to 873. It consisted in building fortifications on both banks of the Seine and in linking them with long wooden bridges. It was only when they were complete, in 873 that the regions around the Seine finally enjoyed a short period of calm. Up to that date, the king was forced to pay increasingly costly Danegelds which, although efficient, had rather perverse effects over time: in 861, the Viking chief Weland, who had settled near the Seine with his men, received 5,000 pounds for driving out a rival band that had taken up position on the island of Oissel. Weland accepted and besieged his rivals, who surrendered over the winter... then he offered to let them stay in exchange for another Danegeld of 6,000 pounds!
The same year, the Viking chief Sygtrygg, also known as Sigfred, left his base on Oissel to lead the third siege of Paris. The following year, Jumièges was totally devastated and the Danes carried off its relics before finally leaving the Seine estuary.

1 Viking sword found in the River Seine between Rouen and Elbeuf (second half of the 9th century).
2 Viking scabbard chape found at Les Mureaux alongside the Seine.
3 Scandinavian percussion lighter found between Vétheuil and Mantes-la-Jolie.
4 Thor's hammer made of silver found in Saint-Pierre-de-Varengeville.
5 Viking axe (second half of the 9th century).

Watercolour by Golvin: Pont-de-l'Arche. Arles Museum of Antiquity.

Charles the Bald then made all efforts to regain control of Aquitaine, which he succeeded in doing in 864, before breaking the alliance between the Bretons and the Loire Vikings. However, his success story came to an end in 866, when the powerful marquis of Neustria, Robert the Strong, was killed during the Battle of Brissarthe, near Le Mans. The Loire Vikings continued their brutality, but with lesser intensity, whilst the Danes in turn concentrated their efforts on the north of England. However, in 876, the foundation of the Danelaw, followed the next year by Charles the Bald's death, paved the way for a new wave of violence. In 879, a "great army" of Danes sailed from England to land near Boulogne, before thrusting inland within the Frankish territory. Two years later, the Vikings were back in the Seine area and, in 885, their chief Sigfred besieged Paris for the fourth time. The following year, a band ravaged Coutances before turning towards Saint-Lô, whilst another ventured as far as Burgundy. In 890, the inhabitants of Saint-Lô were massacred and the Bishop of Coutances was murdered. It was only in 892, after thirteen years of violence, that the great Danish army finally left the Continent...

Excavation in one of the large ditches around the Pont-de-l'Arche fortification.

The four Paris sieges

The Vikings besieged Paris for the first time in 845. Their chief, Ragnar Shaggy Breeches, a semi-legendary king of the seas, commanded a fleet of 120 drakkars, transporting 6,000 warriors. They ransacked the lower Seine then sailed up the river towards the poorly defended city, whose inhabitants fled, whilst a Frankish army took up position before Saint-Denis. But the Vikings crushed them, ravaged Saint-Denis, then Saint-Cloud, and entered Paris on the 28th of March. King Charles the Bald then offered Ragnar 7,000 pounds of silver if he spared the town. The Vikings accepted, but, lured by such booty, they came back three times, in 856, 861 and 885. In 856, they set fire to the monasteries that refused to pay them a Danegeld. In 861, they pillaged Saint-Germain-des-Prés and, after destroying the great Paris bridge over the Seine, captured anyone who tried to escape by boat. Over the following years, Charles the Bald had the bridge rebuilt and fortified the city walls. It proved to be a wise initiative for the town suffered a fourth siege in 885, by an immense army commanded by Sigfred, who established his headquarters in Rouen on the 5th of July, to reach Paris on the 24th of November 885, after successfully passing the Pont-de-l'Arche and Pontoise fortifi-

The siege of Paris - engraving by Alphonse de Neuville taken from *L'Histoire de France* (The History of France) by Guizot, 1883.

cations. The siege, punctuated by violent combat during which Robert the Strong's son, Count Odo, distinguished himself, continued till May 887! Meanwhile, in November 886, Emperor Charles the Fat tried to reroute Sigfred towards Burgundy, after promising him 700 pounds of silver. In vain, for the Vikings, who had succeeded in penetrating inside the town and in destroying the gatehouse, occupied the stronghold until a Danegeld was paid in May 887. In December, Charles the Fat was deposed and Odo, Robert the Strong's son, was crowned King of West Francia in 888. Sigfred in turn continued his career as a Viking until his death during the Battle of Louvain in 891.

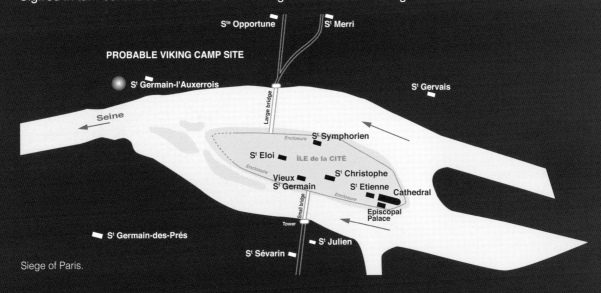

Siege of Paris.

Eastwarðs, the Varangian aðventure

Map of the Varangian routes to the East.

The Vikings of Sweden, referred to as "Varangians", took a different route from their Norwegian and Danish equals: the Baltic route. From the eastern coast of Sweden and the island of Gotland, they sailed towards Slavic lands, before reaching the present-day region of Saint Petersburg, probably in the 750s. The Swedes were already well familiar with the Gulf of Finland and the mouth of the Neva which they sailed up as far as Lake Lagoda, in the heart of Slavic territory.

As they gradually advanced inland, the Varangians established fortified marketplaces, referred to in Russian as *goroda*, which progressively became riverbank merchant towns, such as Staraya Ladoga, Gorodishche and Veliky Novgorod, on the banks of the Volkhov River. Within these towns, the Swedes lived in harmony with the Slavs. It is during the same period, that a new principality is believed to have emerged: Rus' - a political entity that the Varangians continuously extended throughout present-day Russia and the Ukraine up to the mid 9th century. These towns were totally built of timber and local conditions in Northwest Russia have resulted in vestiges from the Varangian period that are remarkably well preserved. Archaeological excavation and dendrochronological dating of its oldest timber constructions have established that Staraya Ladoga, the first marketplace, was founded in 753. Up to around 950, the town was home to one of the largest commercial ports in Eastern Europe. Varangian merchant ships sailed from Sweden to the mouth of the River Neva via the Baltic Sea. They then continued up the River Volkhov to Lake Ladoga, from where the Volga and the Dniepr enabled trade links to be established with Constantinople, the capital of the Byzantine Empire, and beyond, as far as the banks of the Black Sea and the Caspian Sea, trade outlets for caravans from Baghdad and silk-producing countries.

The Staraya Ladoga fortress, 12th century.

Archaeological excavation conducted in the Novgorod region has established the presence of an early urban settlement, *Gorodishche*, the Russian name for a princely residence, which emerged before 850 around three kilometres from Novgorod. It is mentioned for the first time in chronicles dating from 859, under the Old Norse name of Holmgård. At the time, it was home to a fortress belonging to Rurik (circa 830-879), prince of the Varangians and today considered as the very first monarch of what later became Russia. Then in 900, a new town was founded on the outskirts of Gorodishche. Established in the late 10th century, it was initially a group of three villages, within which a kremlin, i.e. a fortified enclosure, was built. It was baptised *Novyj gorod*: "the new town". The site rapidly became the centre of a new trading city associated with a river port where goods were imported from distant lands aboard flat-bottomed boats, capable

The Vikings of Jómsborg

In the 10th century, the Vikings of Jómsborg formed a semi-legendary community of formidable mercenaries. Although their story is almost entirely drawn from legend, several inscriptions on runestones, including those in Sjörup and Karlevi in Sweden, appear to confirm their existence. Their adventures have been related in several sagas, one of which is exclusively devoted to them: the *Jómsvíkinga saga*. It tells the story of a Danish Viking called Palnatóki who, to flee the wrath of King Harald Bluetooth (*Blåtand*, circa 910-986), took exile in Wendish territory, home to a Slavic population on the present-day coast of Poland. In exchange for his promise never to return to Denmark, the king offered him the land of Jóm, in the heart of the Wendish territory, provided he ensured its defence and prosperity. Palnatóki had a fortress built there which he baptised Jómsborg. Although not formally located today, certain historians believe it to have been on the Polish island of Wolin. Within his fortress, he reunited a community of ferocious combatants of Scandinavian and Slavic origin and devoted to worshiping Odin and Thor. To be accepted, these men were required to win a deathly duel against an existing member and to abide by an extremely strict military code, based on the principle of extreme solidarity and perfect equality between combatants.

Every year, the Vikings of Jómsborg participated in a number of battles during which they gained increasing renown. Upon his death, Palnatóki entrusted his authority to Sigvaldi, an exceptionally foolhardy Viking who, in 986, accepted to help King Harald to destroy the fleet of one of his greatest rivals, the turbulent Norwegian jarl Håkon Sigurdsson (circa 937-995). Informed of their allegiance, Håkon sailed towards them with a powerful fleet via the Hjörung strait and succeeded in crushing the Vikings of Jómsborg. Later, the latter resumed their mercenary activities, in England in particular, until the Norwegian King Magnus put a permanent halt to their doings in 1043, by massacring each and every last one of them then by having their fortress destroyed.

Runestone G280 found in Pilgård, on the island of Gotland in Sweden tells the story of a drowning in the Dniepr.

of sailing up and down Russia's major rivers. Novgorod's docks welcomed honey, wax, hemp and fur. Its wealthy population lived a prosperous life, illustrated by the presence of fine objects such as boxwood combs, Mediterranean sponges, crockery from Persia and cloth from Flanders, discovered by Russian archaeologists.

The Varangians from Rus' were traders above all, earning their great wealth from the exchanges they established with southern Russia and the Byzantine region, via the major Russian rivers - the Neva, the Volkhov,

The Varangian Guard, illumination from *Joannis Scylitzae Synopsis Historiarum, Codex Matritensis Graecus* Vitr. 26-2, 12th century.

the Volga and the Dniepr. Thanks to their flat-bottomed boats, they sailed thousands of kilometres up and down these fluvial motorways on their way to the Black Sea, the Caspian Sea and beyond, trading with the Middle East in Baghdad. Evidence has been found of their travels in the form of a great wealth of Arabic coins discovered along the Volga and in the region of Saint Petersburg. The treasures they imported from these distant lands included honey and fur from the Russian forests, silver from Arabian mines, silk from China, transported by caravans along the silk route, etc.

The Varangians were also exceptional warriors. As in the West, some of them hired their services as mercenaries, equally in the Baltic region, on the present-day coast of Poland, as far as the confines of Kievan Rus' and in the Byzantine Empire in Greece. Around 1040, in the port of Athens, Viking mercenaries who were members of the Byzantine Emperor's guard, engraved the following inscription in runes onto a marble lion that was later taken to the Venetian Arsenal:

The burial mounds of the first princes of Rus' along the banks of the Volkhov.

"Håkon with Ulf, Åsmund and Orn, have conquered this port. These men have received large sums because of the revolt led by the Greek people. Dalk was taken prisoner to distant lands. Egil fought in Romania and in Armenia with Ragnar. Upon Harold the Great's orders, Åsmund engraved these runes, helped by Ásgeir, Thorleif, Thord and Ivard, despite opposition from the Greeks."

The aforementioned men were members of the "Varangian Guard", an elite formation officially founded in 988 and comprised of mercenaries from all Scandinavian populations (and later, also of Norman and Anglo-Saxon origin), in charge of the Emperor's personal protection. The great King Harald "the Hard Ruler" (*Hardraada*, circa 1015-1066), of whom we will speak in more detail later, was also part of this unit before taking the throne of Norway.

These individual enlistments did not prevent their increasing commercial rivalry from generating tension between Rus' and Constantinople, which acted as a mandatory intermediary by jealously maintaining the monopoly on exchanges with the Black Sea and the Middle East.

Archaeological excavation in Novgoroð

Initiated in 1932, archaeological excavation in Novgorod is still ongoing today. Although only 2% of the surface area covered by the town has been explored, it is the longest continuous excavation programme ever conducted. This record can be explained in particular by the exceptional conservatory conditions offered by the soil, the depths of which have offered excellent protection to objects of organic origin such as wood, bone, leather, fabric, as well as metal objects, all found intact. Indeed the archaeological occupation levels are peaty, extremely damp and sheltered from air - conditions which prevent both decomposition and corrosion. On this damp and spongy soil, upon which constructions gradually subsided, the Novgorodians placed several subsequent layers of wood flooring, to reach, over the centuries, a thickness of around ten metres. This has enabled archaeologists to date with rare accuracy each layer of occupation, by matching dendrochronology and other dating methods.

The very many archaeological objects discovered in Novgorod include around a thousand manuscripts on rolls of birch bark. These inscriptions, dated back to the 11th-13th centuries, were written in Novgorodian dialect, a variant of the Kievan dialect. This Nordic linguistic origin indicates a predominantly Slavic population from the town's very early days. The Scandinavians consequently formed a relatively limited group which rapidly integrated the Slavic world. This process is most likely very similar to that experienced in Normandy after 911.

Archaeological excavation of a timber house in Staraya Ladoga, July 2009.

In 882, Rurik's heir, Oleg the Seer (before 882-912), undertook to extend Rus' downstream of the Dniepr towards Kiev in the Ukraine. On his way, he captured Smolensk, then had lords brought to him from Kiev - probably two independent Vikings – to have them executed outside the city walls and to replace them with a member of Rurik's clan. Oleg declared Kiev the new capital of Rus' and, henceforth, sought to extend his influence southwards, via Khazar territory. Relationships with Byzantium rapidly deteriorated and, in 907, Oleg decided to trample Constantinople, which the Varangians referred to as Miklagård, "the great town", with a fleet of two thousand ships. The Greeks sustained a bitter defeat and the emperor was coerced into making a pact with Oleg to whom he conceded the right to settle in the town and to freely trade with the Middle East. Over the 10th century, the Varangians from Kiev consolidated their power by imposing their presence among the local people and by bringing to Kiev many immigrants of Swedish and Slavic origin from the Novgorodian territories. Towards the end of the century, their expansion came to a halt in the Steppes of Central Asia and, in 988, Oleg's son Vladimir received a Christian baptism and married the Byzantine Emperor's daughter. At this period in time, the Varangians were no longer Swedes as such, but formed a new people whose culture was largely inspired by Slavic influences.

The Invitation of the Varangians: "Rurik and his brothers arrive in Ladoga", painting by Viktor M. Vasnetsov, before 1912.

The origins of Normandy

Rollo, jarl of the Normans

It was during the 880s that a Viking chief of the name of Hrólfr appeared in the Bay of Seine. Among other campaigns, he took part in the great siege of Paris from 885 to 887, under Sigfred's command. His nickname, Göngu, signified 'the Vagabond', by allusion to his many travels across the globe. The origins of this great explorer with a promising future are, to this day, haloed by legend. Certain Danish sources prior to his lifetime locate his birth in Denmark in 845, whereas the 13th century Icelandic sagas tell of a Norwegian. The majority of historians agree on the second theory. Rollo is believed, more precisely,

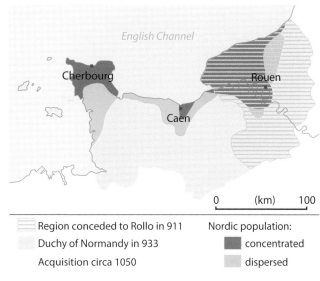

English Channel

Cherbourg

Rouen

Caen

0   (km)   100

Region conceded to Rollo in 911
Duchy of Normandy in 933
Acquisition circa 1050

Nordic population:
concentrated
dispersed

Formation of the duchy of Normandy, 911-1050.

Statue of Rollo in Falaise (Calvados).

ROLLON

to be the son of Rögnvald, the jarl of Møre, a principality located in western-central Norway. In the 860-870s, this Norwegian kinglet set to playing Vikings to the north of the British Isles and settled in Orkney. Furthermore, Snorri Sturluson's Chronicle of the Kings of Norway (*Heimskringla*) relates that Rollo, as many of his contemporaries, was banished from Norway by Harald Fairhair because of his Viking expeditions. He is said to have travelled to England to settle and to launch raids on the continental coast of the North Sea, in command of a motley crew of Danes, Norwegians and Anglo-Saxons.

Rollo and his men then made their entry into the lower Seine region in the early 880s, in the wake of other bands who had almost continuously occupied the area for forty years. They most probably took part in the 885-887 Paris siege, before concentrating on the Bessin area where they challenged the Bretons, who controlled the Cotentin peninsula. In the 11th century, according to the tradition conveyed by Dudo of Saint-Quentin, Normandy's first historian, Rollo is said to have captured the city of Bayeux, by crushing the army led by Count Berengar, a powerful Frankish aristocrat who appears to have been the military chief of a vast territory located on the kingdom's western border, from Bayeux to Le Mans. Since Berengar was killed during the battle, Rollo took his place in Bayeux and married his daughter Poppa. Hence, around 890, our Viking became a powerful and recognised chief, well established in the region of Bayeux, in the confines of the Frankish and Breton king-doms. He benefited from solid alliances with the major Frankish lineages established in the west, from the Bessin to Aqui-taine regions, not forgetting his rear base in England...

It was precisely after a trip to England, during which his son William was born, that Rollo returned to the lower Seine in 898.

The oldest manuscript by Dudo and William of Jumièges, telling of the deeds of the Normans.

Statue of Poppa, Count Berengar's daughter, in Bayeux (Calvados).

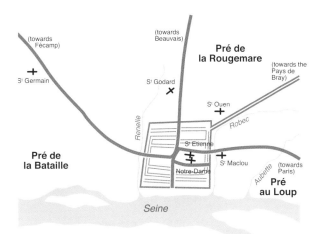

(towards Fécamp)

✝ S¹ Germain

(towards Beauvais)

Pré de la Rougemare

(towards the Pays de Bray)

S¹ Godard ✗

S¹ Ouen ✝

Renelle

Robec

Pré de la Bataille

S¹ Étienne ✝

S¹ Maclou ✝

Notre-Dame

Aubette

(towards Paris)

Pré au Loup

Seine

Map of Rouen in the 10th century.

In Jumièges, he met the king's emissary, the Archbishop of Rouen, whose city he accepted to spare, very probably in exchange for the right to stay there. Historians on early Normandy believe that, by this period, Scandinavian groups had already settled on the banks of the lower Seine, in riverside villages and on the outskirts of Rouen, from the coast to the river's confluence with the Andelle, in the town of Pîtres: such were the frontiers of what was to become the county of Rouen or "early Normandy"...

So, in 911, Rollo was well-established in the lower Seine where he had gathered a powerful Viking army. At the time, he was probably one of the region's first - if not the only - Viking chief, after having eliminated his rivals. He was at the head of several troops established in the sector, including Dives. He then sailed up the Seine and launched a new offensive against Paris. However, strong Frankish opposition led him to reroute towards Chartres, along the River Eure. Nevertheless, the Franks in Neustria and Burgundy joined forces and, once more, succeeded in driving back the Vikings on the 20th of July 911. This unfortunate campaign

Vikings in Dives!

The cartulary by Aganon, Bishop of Chartres during the first half of the 10th century, mentions the presence of Vikings in the Dives estuary in 858, 888 and 911. The site was used as a departure base for pillaging the city of Chartres. Although Aganon attributed these three operations to one unique legendary chief named Hasting, much doubt is to be cast on this theory given the time between the incursions. Their deeds, however, appear to have been the same. As early as 856, the Vikings spent the winter around the Seine, on the island of *Thorholm*, aka Jeufosse or Oissel. The following year, they ransacked Évreux and Chartres, where the Bishop Frobaud died from drowning. In 858, Charles the Bald sent a contingent to dislodge them from their island, but in vain. Mention of the year 888 coincides with a new attack on Paris, after the great 885-887 siege. The same year, the Vikings landed in the Bessin area and headed for Saint-Lô, which was devastated in 890. Finally, during the summer of 911, Rollo in person marched towards Chartres before being arrested by the Franks. It would therefore appear that at least a share of the Vikings engaged in these operations stayed in the Dives estuary, where Carolingian texts mention assets belonging to Jumièges Abbey, including salt mines and cultivated land, a port with fishing rights and a bridge that inspired the site's name: *Pons Divæ* or Pont-Dives.

Portrait of Charles III, known as "the Simple", King of France from 879 to 929, by Georges Rouet, 1838.

offered King Charles the Simple (879-929) a long-awaited opportunity to initiate negotiations with this Viking chief, now far too solidly established within his kingdom for him to chase him out... Charles the Simple therefore sent the Archbishop of Rouen to meet with Rollo and to, on the king's behalf, offer him full property of a land – and not a fief – stretching from the sea to the River Andelle, a territory which coincided precisely with the banks of the lower Seine already occupied by the Vikings. In exchange, Rollo was expected to respect friendly links with Charles, to defend his land against other pretenders, be they the king's Viking or Frankish enemies, and to receive a Christian baptism as godson of Robert (circa 860-923), the chief of the Robertian clan. This final and highly symbolic gesture was not only of religious importance but also had a great political impact: Rollo clearly asserted his integration within the Frankish nobility.

Rollo had very probably also been ready and waiting for a long time. He immediately accepted and the treaty was signed in Saint-Clair-sur-Epte, in the north of the Val-d'Oise. The following year, tradition claims that he was baptised in Rouen Cathedral, adopting his godfather's name: Robert. Such was the birth certificate of the province and the dynasty of Normandy. Also according to tradition, after his baptism, Rollo is said to have officially married Gisela, one of Charles the Simple's daughters; yet, this union, although highly plausible, has never been confirmed by any reliable source.

Rollo did not yet hold the title of duke, but of "jarl of the Normans". This early Normandy was not yet a duchy but a land conceded in full ownership to its new lord, and subject to no political dependence upon the King of West Francia. Rollo was the "prince of the Normans", a title that he and his descendents bore independently of that of Counts of Rouen. Rollo and his men's political integration was a success, for peace was rapidly restored. The jarl of the Normans drove out his Viking

Rollo's baptism by Guy, Archbishop of Rouen. 14th century illumination.

The Treaty of Saint-Clair-sur-Epte on a stained glass window in the town's parish church, by Chanussot, 1913.

rivals to other, less defended lands. As a Christian, or at least officially so, he restored churches and governed in harmony with the Arch-bishop of Rouen. As from the agree-ment they concluded in 890, monks were already able to gradually return to their monasteries and resume their spiritual, intellectual and economic activities. During this period, the city of Rouen became a major marketplace with links, in particular, with southern English ports and with the Vikings' world-wide trade network. The many small ports established along the river-side also enjoyed intense activity,

The Robertian clan

The Robertians, of Frankish origin, owe their name to the fact that very many of their members, who were close to the 7th and 8th century sovereigns, were called Robert. The clan's first illustrious figure was Robert the Strong (815/830-866), Count of Tours and of Anjou, and Marquis of Neustria, who distinguished himself during several battles against the Vikings of the Loire and the Seine. He was killed during one of them, before the church of Brissarthe, in Maine-et-Loire, on the 2nd of July 866. His two sons then succeeded him; firstly the elder, Odo (after 852-898), the hero of the great Paris siege in 885-887, crowned King of Western Francia in 888; then the younger, Robert (circa 860-923) who also acceded to the throne in 922, after deposing Charles the Simple, whose reign was between those of the two brothers. The Robertians were the ancestors of the Capetian dynasty founded by Robert's grandson, Hugh Capet, in 987. The Capetians kept the French throne for eight centuries, from 987 to 1792, then, during the Bourbon Restoration, from 1815 to 1848.

"The death of Robert the Strong", engraving by Paul Lehugeur, 19th century.

Charter by Charles the Simple, drafted in 918 and containing the first written proof of him conceding the region that later became Normandy to Rollo.

many of them adopting new names of Old Norse origin, as groups of Scandinavian immigrants gradually merged with the Frankish population.

After the treaty of Saint-Claire-sur-Epte, Rollo continued his pillaging expeditions in an aim to expand his territory, whilst maintaining his friendship with Charles the Simple. Henceforth, Paris was spared from Viking raids, which most probably earned Rollo support from the Franks of Rouen and the lower Seine, who remained loyal to him, even when the king's power was shadowed by his rivals, up to his deposition in 922. Charles' son, Louis d'Outremer (920/921-954) then fled to England with his mother, Eadgifu of Wessex. In 923, Rollo and his Rouen-based Vikings allied with their compatriots who had settled in the lower Loire, in order to lead a joint northwards expedition that took them as far as Beauvais. By this time, the crown had been passed on to Rudolph of Burgundy (circa 890-936), who, in response to a call from the Robertians, instigated a punitive expedition against Rollo. To his misfortune: the jarl of the Normans launched a powerful counter-attack beyond the Oise region, once more forcing the Franks to pay him a Danegeld, but also to concede to him the lands on the western frontier which he already partly controlled: the Bessin and the Hiémois areas, i.e. all territories located between the Cotentin isthmus and Seine-Maritime.

In 925, Rollo ventured eastwards once more. He landed in the county of Flanders, pillaging Beauvais, Amiens, Arras and Noyon on his way; however, he failed to prevent the Counts of Flanders and Vermandois from taking the fortress of Eu, hence putting paid to his ambitions and establishing, for a long time after, Normandy's frontier on the banks of the River Bresle. Rollo died between 925 and 927, in uncertain circumstances, perhaps after abdicating in favour of his son, William Longsword. The first of the Norman jarls was buried in Rouen Cathedral, but his remains were later transferred to Fécamp Abbey.

Recumbent statue of Rollo, Rouen Cathedral. 14th century.

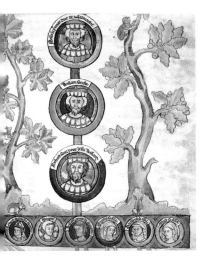

Rollo's descendants, illumination of the manuscript Royal 14 BVI, membrane 5.

From the jarls to the first Dukes of Normandy

From his union with Poppa, his "concubine according to Danish custom" (*frilla more danico*) - even if the Frankish lords did just the same! -, Rollo had at least two children: a daughter, Gerloc, later renamed Adèle, upon her marriage with William Towhead, Count of Poitiers and Duke of Aquitaine; and a son, William, nicknamed Longsword, who succeeded him at the head of the Seine Normans.

William Longsword

The encounter at Picquigny and William Longsword's murder by Arnulf of Flanders in 942. 14th century miniature.

Statue of William Longsword in Falaise (Calvados).

William was born before 910, while his father, in control of the Bessin region, was in England. According to Dudo of Saint-Quentin, Rollo abdicated in his favour in 927, having him proclaimed jarl of the Normans by an assembly of his faithful followers. Indeed, the same year, William recommended himself to King Charles the Simple and officially succeeded his Viking father. A faithful Christian, which Rollo most probably never truly was, William Longsword was very keen to restore churches and to extend his authority towards Cotentin, still in Breton hands. In 931 or 932, a Norman army invaded Brittany, plagued by dissidence and threatened by the Loire Vikings. Hence, King Rudolph received the Norman's homage for the "land of the Bretons located on the banks of the sea", in other words the Cotentin and the Avranchin regions, formerly conceded by Charles the Bald to the Bretons. It was within this troubled context that, in 934, William was to bring to heel a rebellion led by a group of disloyal Vikings, most likely a frequent event in 10th century Normandy. Originating from the west of future Normandy, these men were commanded by Herjólfr, who was better known by the Latinised name of Riouf. Contesting William's legitimacy and his Frankish allegiances, they came to besiege Rouen before being crushed by the jarl's army. Barely had he reasserted his authority, when William took the hand, over a Christian wedding, of the Count of Vermandois' daughter, hence making the first step towards improved relations with the Ponthieu region, whose counts were soon to pay homage to the Norman lord. However, such allegiance aroused concern for the Count of Flanders who, on the 17th of December 942, managed to lure William Longsword into a trap in Picquigny, in the Somme area, where he had him assassinated in cowardly circumstances.

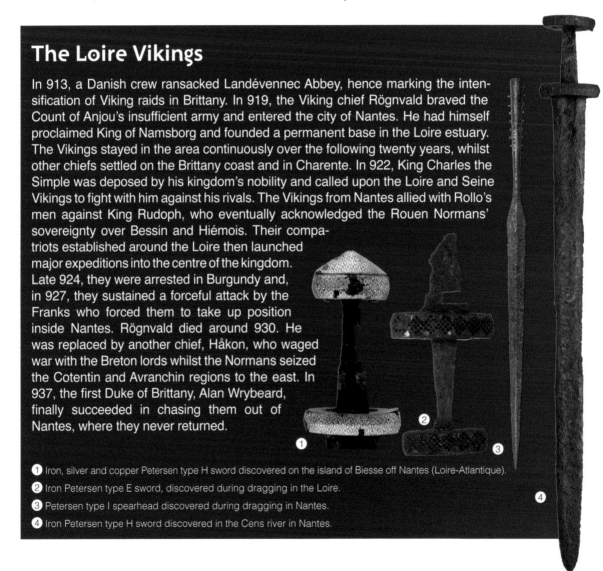

The Loire Vikings

In 913, a Danish crew ransacked Landévennec Abbey, hence marking the intensification of Viking raids in Brittany. In 919, the Viking chief Rögnvald braved the Count of Anjou's insufficient army and entered the city of Nantes. He had himself proclaimed King of Namsborg and founded a permanent base in the Loire estuary. The Vikings stayed in the area continuously over the following twenty years, whilst other chiefs settled on the Brittany coast and in Charente. In 922, King Charles the Simple was deposed by his kingdom's nobility and called upon the Loire and Seine Vikings to fight with him against his rivals. The Vikings from Nantes allied with Rollo's men against King Rudoph, who eventually acknowledged the Rouen Normans' sovereignty over Bessin and Hiémois. Their compatriots established around the Loire then launched major expeditions into the centre of the kingdom. Late 924, they were arrested in Burgundy and, in 927, they sustained a forceful attack by the Franks who forced them to take up position inside Nantes. Rögnvald died around 930. He was replaced by another chief, Håkon, who waged war with the Breton lords whilst the Normans seized the Cotentin and Avranchin regions to the east. In 937, the first Duke of Brittany, Alan Wrybeard, finally succeeded in chasing them out of Nantes, where they never returned.

1 Iron, silver and copper Petersen type H sword discovered on the island of Biesse off Nantes (Loire-Atlantique).
2 Iron Petersen type E sword, discovered during dragging in the Loire.
3 Petersen type I spearhead discovered during dragging in Nantes.
4 Iron Petersen type H sword discovered in the Cens river in Nantes.

Richard I

William Longsword's tragic death left but a small boy of ten years to succeed him: Richard, known as "the Fearless", born from his *frilla* Sprota, who may have been a Breton princess. Richard was immediately placed under the protection of regents selected among the great Norman lords; however, King Louis IV d'Outremer ordered for Richard to be brought to his court in Laon, accompanied by one of his tutors, Osmond de Conteville, on the pretext of his wish to perfect the child's education. In truth, the young Norman was held hostage. Louis IV immediately placed Normandy under the Count of Ponthieu's control, before invading the province. The Normans from Rouen then called upon two Viking chiefs, a Norwegian called Sigtrygg and a pagan Norman, Turmod, who were both defeated by the Franks. The situation grew increasingly bitter until, in 945, Bernard the Dane, one of Richard's tutors, called upon another Viking chief called Hagrold, most probably one of the "kings of the sea" who had settled on the Normandy coast, making a living from warfare...

Mid-July 95, Hagrold's Vikings landed in the Dives estuary, at the locality referred to as "la Saline de Corbon", "where the rapid stream of the Dives flows into the sea" according to Dudo, on the banks of the small port of Dives-sur-Mer, near the wooden bridge that crossed the river. On this spot, Viking mercenaries joined Bernard the Dane's Normans and they set off to challenge a Frankish detachment led by

Statue of Richard I in Falaise (Calvados).

the king himself. They had arrived in Dives-sur-Mer the previous evening, taking up position on the opposite bank. The Normans crossed the River Dives, probably over the bridge, then Hagrold and Louis marched towards each other. The Vikings suddenly engaged in combat! The Count of Ponthieu, Normandy's governor, fell with several of his men and Louis d'Outremer was captured. The ransom for his freedom was Richard's acknowledgment as Duke of Normandy.

Charter by William the Conqueror in favour of Fécamp Abbey, 1085.

Gunnor making a donation to the Mont Saint-Michel. Avranches municipal library, Ms. 201, 12th century

The following year, Louis IV reunited a coalition force and marched towards Rouen once more. Yet, Norman resistance forced him to retreat. In 947, by which time the Scandinavian foundations in the Danelaw and around the Loire had been annihilated, Richard the Fearless became the first official Duke of Normandy. He continued his father's political efforts, succeeding in thwarting the king's and the Frankish lords' ambitions, submitting the established Viking chiefs to the west of the duchy, forging friendly links with England, establishing bishops in all the cathedrals throughout his duchy, building a palace in Fécamp and commissioning the Saint-Quentin monk Dudo to write the *Deeds of the Norman Dukes (Gesta Normannorum Ducum)*. Around 960, in order to seal his status in the king's eyes, Richard took Emma of France, Hugh Capet's daughter, as his wife during a Christian marriage. A few years later, Hugh Capet in turn married a princess

of Norman origin: Adelaide, Rollo's granddaughter on her mother Adèle's side. Five years later, peace was finally concluded with the king, who agreed to no longer call the Norman frontiers into question. Equally eager to consolidate his allegiance with the "kings of the sea", Richard also married "Scandinavian style" a high-ranking Danish princess: Gunnor, who was a descendent of King Gorm the Old, whom we spoke of earlier, and the sister of Herfast of Crépon, father of the future Seneschal Osbern who lost his life while saving young William the Bastard. After Emma's death in 968, Richard's *frilla more danico* became his first wife. Since Emma had left no descendents, Gunnor was to give birth to the heir of the duchy, baptised with his father's name, and to Emma aka Ælfgifu, who later became Queen of England and of Denmark after her successive marriages with Æthelred II (†1016), Edward the Confessor's father, then Canute the Great (†1035). It was by her intervention that William the Bastard had a legitimate claim to the throne of England, due to his family ties with King Edward...

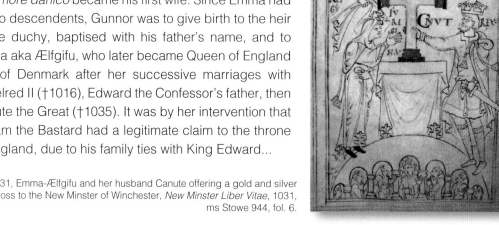

In 1031, Emma-Ælfgifu and her husband Canute offering a gold and silver cross to the New Minster of Winchester, *New Minster Liber Vitae*, 1031, ms Stowe 944, fol. 6.

Richard II

Richard I died in 996, the same year as Hugh Capet. He was buried in Fécamp and, once more, his young heir saw his power contested. This succession crisis was aggravated by a peasant rebellion, which was quickly repressed over a bloodbath by Richard's uncle, Rodulf, who also intervened to keep other pretenders at bay. During this difficult minority, Gunnor and Rodulf managed to impose Richard's authority. Once firmly established as duke, Richard consolidated Normandy's administration by founding the "Richardide" clan and by more clearly adopting a Frankish model, to the detriment of Scandinavian customs. His strategy was deployed via closer links with King Louis the Pious (778-840), who was very much in need of allies to thwart the Frankish counts' ambitions. In contrast, in no way did this prevent the Norman from establishing other chosen alliances, which he reinforced by marrying off his sisters and by, himself, taking the hand of Judith, the Duke of Brittany's sister. He also readily called upon as many "kings of the sea" as necessary. From Rouen, they launched Viking raids on the coasts of France, Spain and England, embarking Norman contingents aboard their ships. Some of them were important figures, for example - in 1014 - the future King of Norway, St. Olaf (circa 995-1030), descended from Harald Fairhair and who was baptised in Rouen. At the time, the town was a major Viking port, including a slave market and with links with the leading Northern European marketplaces in the hands of the Scandinavian kings. Furthermore, during the same period, Norman horsemen were available for hire for expeditions as far as southern Italy, where they even fought against the Byzantine Emperor's Varangian Guard!

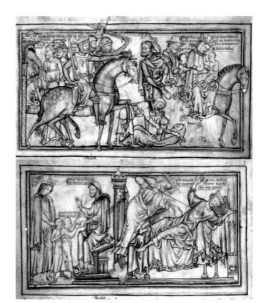

Emma and her sons fled to England to seek refuge in Richard II's court. *La Estoire de Seint Aedward le Rei* (Life of Edward the Confessor), circa 1250, ms Ee359, f°4 and 4v, 13th century.

Saint Olaf, illumination from the Jónsbók, Arnamagnæanske Institute, Copenhagen.

In 1001, this activity infuriated the King of England, Æthelred II, known as "the Unready" (866/968-1016) – we will see why – who, in retaliation, despatched an army to Réville in the Val de Saire, where it was annihilated. The following year, Richard tried to diplomatically resolve their quarrels by offering Æthelred his sister Emma's hand. The king accepted, however, determined to be done with the Vikings, he made a terrible decision that was to prove fatal: on the 13th of November 1002, on St. Brice's day, he ordered for the Danes of the Danelaw to be massacred...

Portrait of Louis the Pious by Jean-Joseph Dassy, 1837.

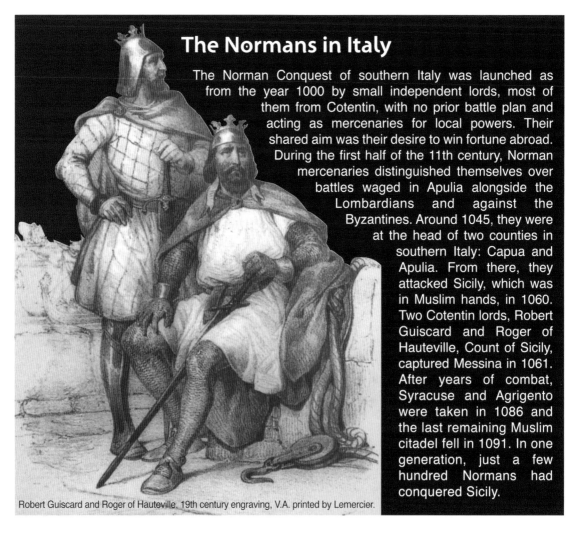

The Normans in Italy

The Norman Conquest of southern Italy was launched as from the year 1000 by small independent lords, most of them from Cotentin, with no prior battle plan and acting as mercenaries for local powers. Their shared aim was their desire to win fortune abroad. During the first half of the 11th century, Norman mercenaries distinguished themselves over battles waged in Apulia alongside the Lombardians and against the Byzantines. Around 1045, they were at the head of two counties in southern Italy: Capua and Apulia. From there, they attacked Sicily, which was in Muslim hands, in 1060. Two Cotentin lords, Robert Guiscard and Roger of Hauteville, Count of Sicily, captured Messina in 1061. After years of combat, Syracuse and Agrigento were taken in 1086 and the last remaining Muslim citadel fell in 1091. In one generation, just a few hundred Normans had conquered Sicily.

Robert Guiscard and Roger of Hauteville. 19th century engraving, V.A. printed by Lemercier.

Upon news of the carnage, the King of Denmark, Sweyn Forkbeard (*Tyvskæg*, v. 960-1014) was wild with fury! In 1003, he landed a fleet and invaded England. Ten years later, Æthelred, Emma and their sons Edward and Alfred owed their salvation exclusively to Richard who welcomed them to Fécamp. They stayed there until Sweyn's death the following year. Nevertheless, Æthelred did not survive the Danes for long. When he passed away in London, on the 23rd of April 1016, the crown was to be passed on to his son Edmund Ironside (circa 988-1016). Yet, Sweyn's son, Canute the Great (994/995-1035), a fearsome warrior who may have been a member of the Jómsborg Viking family, also claimed the crown. He landed in Kent with two hundred ships on the 18th of October 1016 and crushed Edmund's troops at the Battle of Assandun in southeast Essex. He conquered virtually the entire kingdom, with the exception of Wessex until, a few days later, Edmund died in obscure circumstances. Canute was still a pretender. He kidnapped Emma before assuming the crown and Richard II had no choice but to reluctantly acknowledge the new king, whilst continuing to offer King Æthelred's sons shelter within his palace. In July 1017, Canute and Emma's wedding was officially celebrated then the Danes' maritime power increased by huge proportions: in 1018, Canute succeeded his father to the throne of Denmark then, ten years later, took the crown of Norway. He was to receive the very last official Danegeld ever paid in the history of the English Vikings: a colossal treasure of 82,500 pounds! The same year, his fleet returned to Denmark with a fabulous booty... and no one dared to disturb it...

Upon Richard's death in August 1026, early Normandy was transformed into a powerful and radiant principality. It was united by close relations with the major figures of the Frankish kingdom and of England, Denmark and Norway. The Viking raids had ceased for almost a decade, the last stir recorded in history dating back to 1017. The duke officially designated his elder son Richard as his successor, entrusting the County of Hiémois to his younger son Robert.

Æthelred II, known as "the Unready" (866/968-1016). Illumination from the Abingdon Chronicle, circa 1220, British Library, London, ms Cotton Claude BVI, fol 87v.

Richard III and Robert the Magnificent

Young Richard III, associated with the ducal power since his very childhood, was first to subject his brother who he then upheld as Count of Hiémois. In 1027, he married Adèle, the very young daughter of Robert the Pious (circa 972-1031). But his time was too short to offer her children: Richard III died on the 6th of August the same year, very probably due to poisoning organised by his own brother. He was buried in the church of Saint-Ouen in Rouen and, a year later, Adèle remarried with Count Baldwin V of Flanders (1012-1067). From their union in 1032, Matilda, future spouse and also cousin of William the Bastard, was born.

Robert I, known as "the Liberal" or "the Magnificent" (circa 1010-1035) was proclaimed duke in August 1027, at the age of 17. His first priority was to subject his rivals, including the powerful Archbishop of Rouen and Count of Évreux, Robert the Dane. Then he established political and military allegiances with the King of France Henry I (1008-1060) and the Count of Flanders, Baldwin IV (980-1035), before subjugating Brittany. With Canute the Great, relations evolved in a different manner for Robert had cut his father's diplomatic links and demanded that the Danes return their crown to its rightful heirs Æthelred and Robert's sister Emma.

Statue of Richard III in Falaise (Calvados).

Canute refused categorically and the enraged duke decided to arm a fleet of warships to land in England! In 1033, the Norman ships set sail from Fécamp, but the historian William of Jumièges, the only one to relate the event, tells of the ships drifting due to a storm and the operation turning into a fiasco. It is said to have ended with a raid towards Jersey and the Mont Saint-Michel bay... Whatever happened, there is no doubt that this failed encounter was still fresh in William the Bastard's memory in 1066.

Within the duchy, Robert owed his name to the many formerly usurped assets he returned to monasteries and to the foundations he personally chaired in Carisy, in 1032, and in Montivilliers in 1035, emulated by his followers. A little later, Robert decided to make a pilgrimage to the Holy Land, possibly riddled with guilt for having murdered his brother. Before leaving, he reunited his court in Fécamp on the 13th of January, and officially named his son William, aged 7 years, as his successor should he pass away. Robert reached Jerusalem but died on his return journey, in Nicaea, during the summer of 1035, perhaps poisoned...

Statue of Robert the Magnificent in Falaise (Calvados).

William the Bastard

William the Bastard was the son of Robert and his *frilla*, Herleva – also known as Arlette – whose father was a rich burgher from Falaise named Foubert. Very close to the duke, he was his valet at Falaise Castle and, as such, looked after his audiences, his treasure and good living at the palace. We can reasonably suppose that he made his fortune from the fur trade, hence the nickname "tanner" which William's enemies attributed to him. Some have even suggested he may have been an embalmer, a profession which was just as poorly looked upon in the Middle Ages!

As soon as news of his father's death came, William was immediately in great danger. The great Norman lords and pretenders to Robert's succession were surely not going to burden themselves with this young bastard, born from a common girl... However, Arlette was not just Robert's *frilla*. Around 1030, she celebrated a Christian marriage with a lord from Risle, one of the duke's faithful followers: Herluin de Conteville, to whom she gave two sons, William's half brothers: Odo, future Bishop of Bayeux and Robert, future Count of Mortain. Henceforth, the Conteville clan looked after William's protection with help from the barons who had kept their oath to Robert. Gilbert de Brionne, Count of Eu, was William's first tutor and one of the most powerful barons in Normandy. However, he was soon assassinated by order of Ralph of Gacé who, immediately, had himself named Constable of Normandy and took command of the ducal army against his rivals. The young duke's other tutors were also eliminated: firstly Turold, then Seneschal Osbern, who was killed in Vaudreuil as he protected William against murderers who had managed to enter his bedroom. Until 1042, Normandy was prey to successive rebellions and civil war...

Statue of William the Conqueror on horseback in Falaise (Calvados).

Falaise Castle, William the Bastard's birthplace.

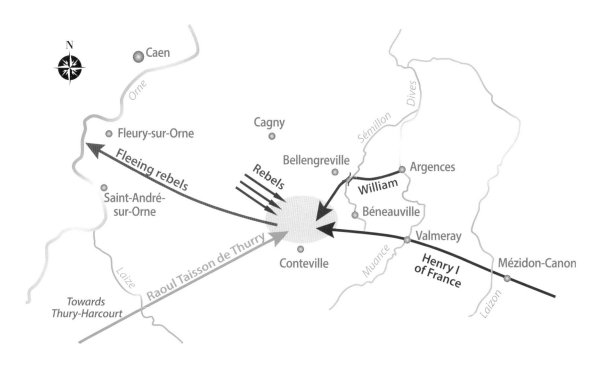

Plan of the Battle of Val-ès-Dunes.

William was dubbed at the age of 14 or 15. In 1046, he only just escaped another murder attempt at Valognes castle. He took refuge in Falaise, reunited his faithful horsemen and called upon the King of France who, in virtue of his homage to William as duke, owed him support against his enemies. In the spring of 1047, Henry I, most likely driven by other motives, personally led a contingent along the banks of the Muance near Argences. The conspirators came to face them the next day: then followed the Battle of Val-ès-Dunes, during which William demonstrated his talents as a warlord for the very first time. Put to rout, his adversaries were harassed into the River Orne at rising tide where they drowned. William then took control of his duchy and restored peace.

BRIONNE. - Ruines du Vieux Château

Postcard of the ruins of the Brionne keep (Eure).

William and Matilda – cousins?

Celebrated in Eu in 1050 or 1051, in surprising privacy, the marriage between William the Bastard and Matilda, the daughter of Count Baldwin IV of Flanders, raised much controversy because of the Pope's interdict proclaimed the previous year during the Council of Reims. His opposition was motivated by the couple's consanguinity which was contradictory to canon law. It was a relatively complex affair for Matilda and William had family links at several different levels. Firstly, they were both Rollo's descendents and, as such, were fifth cousins. However, they were also both considered to be descendents of Richard II, William directly, and Matilda on the side of her grandmother Eleanor, daughter of Richard II and second wife of Count Baldwin IV, who was Baldwin V's father and therefore Matilda's grandfather. Yet, even if Baldwin V was born from his father's first marriage, because Eleanor was his father's second wife, according to canon law, Eleanor's granddaughter was William's third cousin! Finally, Richard II had married Adèle, the very young daughter of the King of France, Robert the Pious, with whom he had no children. However, after Richard's death, Adèle remarried Baldwin V, Matilda's father. In the eyes of the Church, this was also grounds for the interdict. It is of traditional belief that the construction of the two abbeys in Caen, devoted to St. Stephen and the Holy Trinity, also known as the Men's Abbey and the Ladies' Abbey, helped to appease the Pope's wrath.

Portraits of William and Matilda.

Then came the time to think of wedlock... William had set his sights on Matilda, the Count of Flanders' daughter and William's cousin. Despite the interdict stipulated by canon law, the political stakes involved in their union prevailed and their marriage was celebrated in Eu, in 1050 or 1051, in the strictest privacy. William now had a powerful ally – his father-in-law, who was one of the most influential lords on the banks of the English Channel and the North Sea. Such alliance was necessary for William's project.

William was indeed the nephew of the King of England, Edward the Confessor, in turn a descendent of Richard I by the latter's daughter Emma, who remarried with Canute the Great, after the death of Æthelred the Unready. Reviving his father's dream, at the age of 23, William saw the potential for a great future. For his uncle, who, in 1042, had succeeded Canute's son

Harthacanute, still recalled the assistance he was once offered by the dukes of Normandy to the king's fleeing heirs. He had taken care to place his kingdom's high offices in the hands of Normans, to the detriment of the Anglo-Saxons and their chief, Harold Godwinson (circa 1022-1066), Earl of Wessex after his father's death in 1053, who had already set his sights on the crown. During the period from 1051 to 1052, Harold and his brothers took up arms, the conflict only being briefly interrupted by their sister Edith's marriage with Edward. Edward then decided to hand over his crown to William of Normandy...

Edward the Confessor.
Illumination from the manuscript Royal 14 BVI, membrane 4.

Over the same years, William was keen to extend his frontiers. After the King of France himself, his worst enemy was Geoffrey Martel, the Count of Anjou. In 1055, William waged war against the Angevin region and his success was of concern to the King of France who, in 1053, betrayed him and allied with Geoffrey Martel to attack Normandy on two fronts. Despite what was a huge threat, the Normans, led by Gauthier Giffard, crushed the French at Mortemer-sur-Eaulne, in the Pays de Bray. In March 1057, the Franco-Angevins repeated their offensive from Maine. They left Saint-Pierre-sur-Dives to head for Caen, before turning back towards Dives, via Bavent, laden with spoils. Lying in wait on the Varaville road, William set up an ambush. He allowed the enemy to reach the road at level with the wooden bridge that crossed the Dives. Then, as the tide rose, he charged their rear guard, sending many men into the river. The bridge collapsed and the king, who was at the foot of the Basse-bourg hill, helplessly watched his troops drown! Neither Henry I nor Geoffrey Martel returned to Normandy. In 1060, the king died and his regency was entrusted to the Count of Flanders, William's father-in-law. Geoffrey Martel died the same year. The time had come to think of England...

GEOFFROY DIT MARTEL COMTE D'ANIOV, ET DEPVIS RELIGIEVX DE SAINT NICOLAS d'Angers, Principal MINISTRE sous le Roy HENRY I.

Engraved portrait of Geoffrey Martel, Count of Anjou. 17th century.

1066 the end of the Vikings

On the evening of the 14th of October, the Duke of Normandy, descended from a Viking chief known as Göngu-Hrólfr, alias Rollo the Vagabond, himself the son of an obscure Norwegian jarl who had settled in Orkney in the north of Scotland, took the crown of England over armed combat. Hence, he succeeded a long line of Anglo-Saxon kings, but also of Viking sovereigns from Denmark and Norway. Just like the expeditions that took the Northmen as far as Russia and America, the Conquest of England was a great maritime and warring enterprise. And just like his Viking ancestors, William the Conqueror was most probably neither worse nor better than his contemporaries. His renown has taken quite a different tone on either side of the English Channel, an ambiguity shared with all Viking chiefs in general. Although a Frankish and Christian leader, won over by the ideals and customs of his peers, his success was undeniably, first and foremost, due to his extraordinary command of both maritime conditions and his warfaring tactics based on cunning and surprise, quintessential qualities among all Vikings and a long way from the emerging ideals associated with knighthood. The ships, manoeuvres and gestures depicted on the

William the Conqueror's seal, 11th century.

Bayeux Tapestry, an inestimable masterpiece embroidered in England over the ten to fifteen years that followed the event, are direct evidence of the Vikings' fascinating maritime legacy. For many reasons, and not only for their indisputable violence, these great explorers from the North, who ventured far afield to encounter their contemporaries have collectively forged European history, leaving their mark in many a land, among which Normandy.

Photo credits

Detail of the Bayeux Tapestry – 11th century - With special permission from Bayeux Town Council. p. 7, 8, 11, 38-bottom, 48, 49-bottom-left • Photographs by C. Le Callonec: p. 9, 12, 13 • Photograph by H. Paitier, Inrap: p. 10 • Photographs by Wikimedia Commons: p. 14, 18, 20, 21, 22-top, 24, 26-top, 28, 30, 33, 36, 38-top, 41-top, 42, 44-bottom-left, 44-bottom, 47-top, 49-bottom, 52, 53, 54, 55, 56-bottom, 57-bottom, 60-bottom, 61, 62, 63 left, 64-bottom, 65-bottom, 71, 72, 74, 75, 76-left, 78, 80- bottom, 81, 84, 86, 87, 88, 89 • Museum of Fine Arts, Caen, M. Seyve photographer: p. 16 • © Fotolia – Thomas Owen: p. 17 • © Dives-sur-Mer Town Council: p. 19 • Stockholm National Museum of Antiquities. Photograph by S.C. Bikel: p. 22-bottom • Excavation by Oxford Archaeology, Photograph courtesy of Dorset County Council: p. 23 • Paris, BnF (National Library of France): p. 25, 92-bottom • National and University Library of Iceland, ms IB2994to: p. 26-bottom • Photograph by V. Carpentier: p. 27, 66, 70-bottom, 73 • Watercolours by Jean-Claude Golvin. Musée départemental Arles Antique © Jean-Claude Golvin / Éditions Errance: p. 34, 68-top • Árni Magnússon Institute, Reykjavík: p. 35, 57-left • Gotland Museum, Visby, Sweden. Rights reserved: p. 37 • British Museum, London: p. 40, 64-top • The Viking Ship Museum, Oslo: p. 41-bottom, 43-top • The Viking Ship Museum, Oslo, Photograph by W. Karrasch: p. 43-bottom • Photography Yohann Deslandes © Museum of Antiquities, Rouen; p. 44-top, 67 • The Viking Ship Museum, Roskilde: p. 45, 46-top, 47-centre • The Viking Ship Museum, Roskilde. Photograph by Don Hitchcock: p. 46-bottom • The Viking Ship Museum, Roskilde, Photograph by B. Asmussen: p. 46-bottom bas • Swedish History Museum, Stockholm: p. 49-centre • Isaacs Art Center Museum and Gallery, Waimea, Hawaï Islands, USA: p. 54 • Photograph by M. Church, Durham University: p. 56-top • Arnamagnæan Institute, University of Copenhagen, Denmark: p. 59-top • Photograph by C.-K. Masden, rights reserved: p. 59-bottom • National Museum of Scotland, rights reserved: p. 60-top • National Museum of Antiquities, Leiden: p. 65-top • Photograph by C. Marcigny, Inrap: p. 68-bottom • © Municipal Library of Rouen: p. 76-right • Abbey of Saint-Germain-des-Prés, Centre historique des Archives nationales (French national archives): p. 80-top • © Photograph by C. Hémon, Dobrée Museum (Nantes) and heritage sites – Grand patrimoine de Loire-Atlantique, inv. 928.2.1 : p. 82, no 1 • © Photograph by C. Letertre, Dobrée Museum (Nantes) and heritage sites - Grand patrimoine de Loire-Atlantique, inv. 930.1.884 : p. 82, no 4 • © Photograph by C. Letertre, Dobrée Museum (Nantes) and heritage sites – Grand patrimoine de Loire-Atlantique, inv. 878.2.1 : p. 82, no 2 • © Photograph by H. Neveu-Dérotrie, Dobrée Museum (Nantes) and heritage sites - Grand patrimoine de Loire-Atlantique, inv. 930.1.866 : p. 82, no 3 • Seine-Maritime departmental archives, 7H2151: p. 83-bottom • Cambridge University Library: p. 85-top • Photograph by S. Reitz, E.L. Pedersen: p. 85-bottom • Municipal Library of Caen: p. 91 • British Library: p. 92-top • Paris, National Archives: p. 93.

Bibliography

Borja & Miniac, *Guillaume, bâtard et conquérant*, (comic strip), Editions OREP, 2014.

Boyer Régis, *Snorri Sturluson* – Le plus grand écrivain islandais du Moyen Âge, (coll. « Héritages vikings »), éditions OREP, 2012.

Carpentier Vincent, *Guillaume le Conquérant et l'estuaire de la Dives*. Les coulisses d'une conquête, Association Le Pays d'Auge, 2011.

Carpentier Vincent et Ladune Vincent, *Guillaume de Normandie*. La jeunesse de Guillaume le Conquérant, Lisieux, Association Le Pays d'Auge, 2013, illustrated book.

Carpentier Vincent, *Les Vikings à petits pas*, Actes-Sud/Inrap, 2016.

Fettu Annie, *Guillaume le Conquérant*, éditions OREP, republished in 2015.

Hourquet M., Pivard G. et Sehier J.-F., *Guillaume le Conquérant – Sur les chemins de l'histoire*, éditions OREP, 2015.

Lajoye Patrice, *Mythes et légendes scandinaves*, (coll. « Héritages vikings »), éditions OREP, 2011.

Lemagnen Sylvette, *La Tapisserie de Bayeux – Une découverte pas à pas*, éditions OREP, 2015.

Renaud Jean, *La Normandie des Vikings*, éditions OREP, 2008.

Renaud Jean (dir.), *L'épopée viking*, éditions OREP, 2005.

Renaud Jean, *Les Vikings et les patois de Normandie et des îles Anglo-Normandes*, éditions OREP, 2008.

Ridel Elisabeth, *Les Navires de la Conquête – Construction navale et navigation en Normandie à l'époque de Guillaume le Conquérant*, (coll. « Héritages vikings »), éditions OREP, 2010.

Ridel Elisabeth, *Paroles de Vikings – Dictionnaire des mots issus de l'ancien scandinave dans les parlers de Normandie et des îles Anglo-Normandes*, (coll. « Héritages vikings »), éditions OREP, 2012.

Ridel Elisabeth (dir.), *Les Vikings dans l'empire franc*, (coll. « Héritages vikings »), éditions OREP, 2014.

ISBN : 978-2-8151-0317-6
© **OREP Éditions 2016**
All rights reserved - **Legal deposit:** 2nd quarter 2016